W9-CPF-571

POMPEII

History and Art
The New Archaeological Areas
Map of the Excavations

PLEASE SEE PAGES 2-5 FOR ITINERARIES

>─┼─❯❯─O─❮┼❮

Distributed by:

d'ORIANO editore s.r.l.
www.dorianoeditore.it
Via A. Diaz, 20 Pompei (Na)
Tel. 081/8631010

ITINERARIES FOR VISITING THE SITE

*Entrance to the archaeological area of Pompeii is from **Porta Marina**, **Piazza Esedra** or **Piazza Anfiteatro**.*
A visit to the entire complex requires at least one day.
For those whose time is limited, some highlights are indicated below, starting at Porta Marina and Piazza Esedra or at Piazza Anfiteatro, with numbers that refer to the buildings to be visited.
Due to the ongoing work of restoration and reorganization, some of the buildings described in this book may at times be closed to the public.

PORTA MARINA

This was the western entrance to the city, facing towards the sea and one of the most impressive gates, though originally not one of the most used. Today it is one of the main entrances to the archaeological excavations, though it is not entirely convenient given the steep slope of the land here. On the outside are bars, the information office, audio-guides as well as the ticket office and the luggage deposit. Nearby is the Circumvesuviana train station, on the Naples-Sorrento line.

PIAZZA ESEDRA

The modern and recently created entrance located at Piazza Esedra provides a quite fascinating approach to the excavations. Surrounded by the flourishing vegetation along Viale delle Ginestre we arrive directly into the heart of the buried city.

Porta Marina and Piazza Esedra entrance

Suggestions for a 2-hour visit

1 4 5 8 10 11 12 13 14 16 17 20 22 28 29 31 32 34 45 46 61 62 63

Suggestions for a 4-hour visit

1 4 5 7 8 10 11 12 13 14 17 19 20 22 28 29 31 32 34 45 46 55 57 61 62 63 67 72 77 85 86 90 97

PIAZZA ANFITEATRO

The southern entrance to Pompeii is here, broad, convenient and situated in a leafy and shaded area with open spaces flanking the interesting area of necropolis at Porta Nocera. A ticket office and the luggage deposit are also available here for the visitor. Nearby is the Circumvesuviana train station, on the Naples-Poggiomarino line.

Piazza Anfiteatro entrance

Suggestions for a 2-hour visit

61 62 63 67 71 72 75 76 82 84 85 86 87 89 90 91 94 95 96 97

Suggestions for a 4-hour visit

8 10 11 12 13 14 20 29 31 32 61 62 63 67 69 70 71 72 73 75 76 79 81 82 83 84 85 86 87 89 90 91 94 95 96 97

WHAT TO SEE IN POMPEII

EXCAVATIONS OF POMPEII

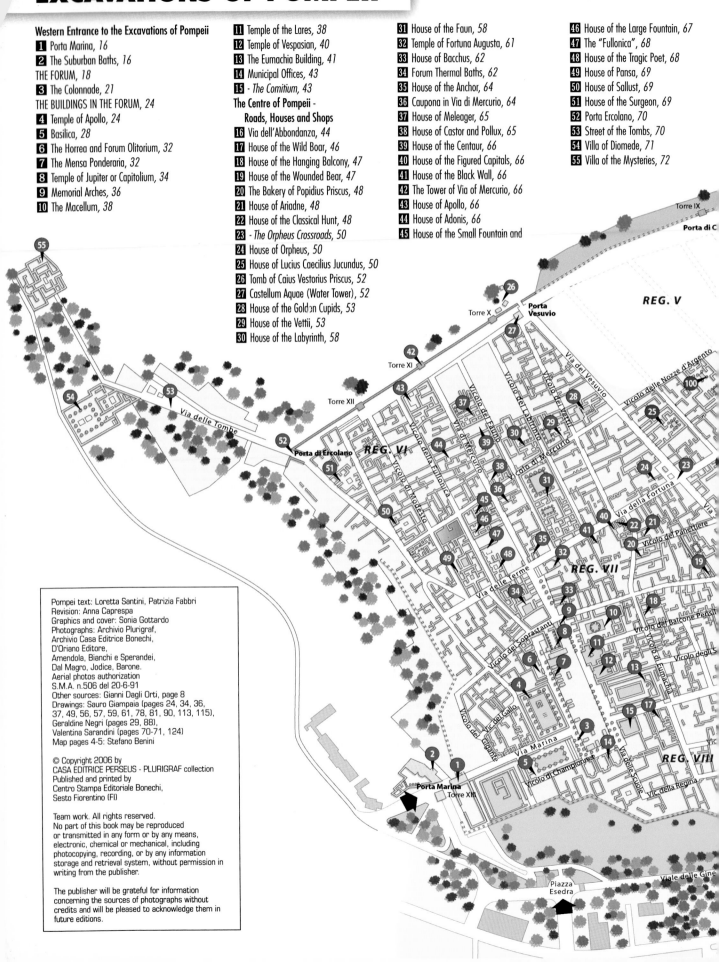

Pompei text: Loretta Santini, Patrizia Fabbri
Revision: Anna Caprespa
Graphics and cover: Sonia Gottardo
Photographs: Archivio Plurigraf,
Archivio Casa Editrice Bonechi,
D'Oriano Editore,
Amendola, Bianchi e Sperandei,
Dal Magro, Jodice, Barone.
Aerial photos authorization
S.M.A. n.506 del 20-6-91
Other sources: Gianni Dagli Orti, page 8
Drawings: Sauro Giampaia (pages 24, 34, 36,
37, 49, 56, 57, 59, 61, 78, 81, 90, 113, 115),
Geraldine Negri (pages 29, 88),
Valentina Sarandini (pages 70-71, 124)
Map pages 4-5: Stefano Benini

© Copyright 2006 by
CASA EDITRICE PERSEUS - PLURIGRAF collection
Published and printed by
Centro Stampa Editoriale Bonechi,
Sesto Fiorentino (FI)

Team work. All rights reserved.
No part of this book may be reproduced
or transmitted in any form or by any means,
electronic, chemical or mechanical, including
photocopying, recording, or by any information
storage and retrieval system, without permission in
writing from the publisher.

The publisher will be grateful for information
concerning the sources of photographs without
credits and will be pleased to acknowledge them in
future editions.

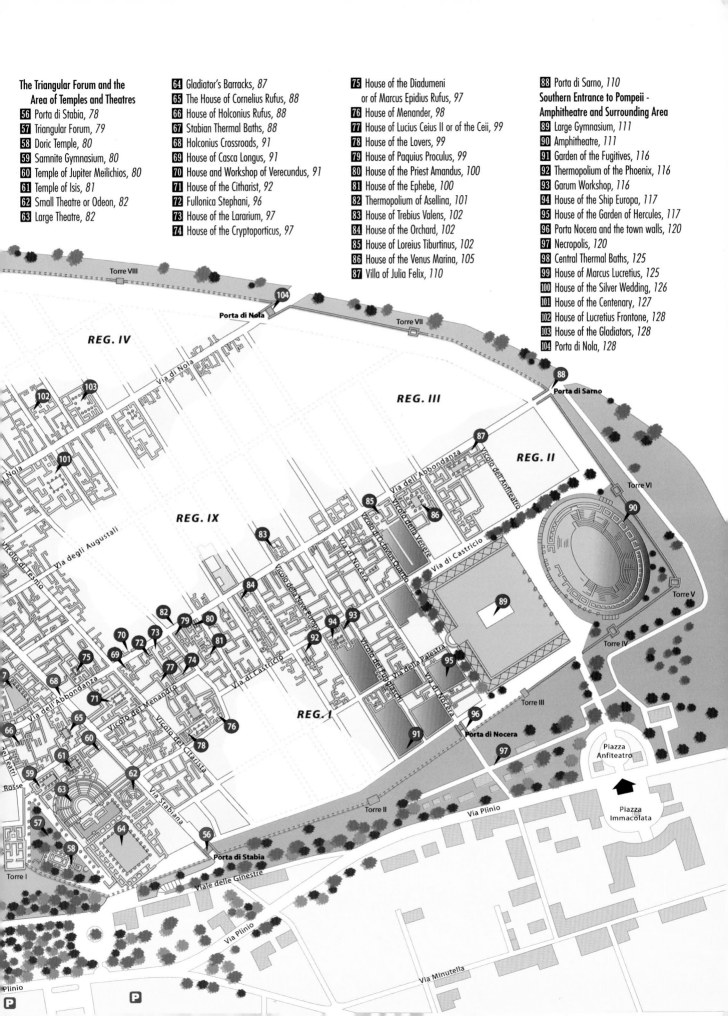

P ompeii, unlike the other towns in Campania that were mainly founded by Greek colonists, was built by the Oscans, probably around the 9-8th century B.C., although the evidence currently available dates no further back than the 6th century.

The town developed on terraces of lava formed many centuries earlier. It constituted an important natural defence against the threat of invasion by neighbouring peoples. At the same time, the volcanic nature of the land meant the territory of the Sarno valley was particularly fertile, thereby allowing for the rapid development of the agricultural economy.

Pompeii soon made contact with the nearby Greek colonies, whose culture, way of life and the religion of Magna Graecia it quickly absorbed. Evidence of this is to be found in the shape of the Doric temple which stands in the Triangular Forum.

The city was governed by the Etruscans for almost fifty years (until 474 B.C.) when the latter occupied part of inland Campania. Immediately afterwards it returned to the Greek sphere of influence.

It then became part of the Samnite area of expansion (5th century), and experienced remarkable growth during this period when the historical centre, whose remains are still visible, was formed. This can be identified in part of the most ancient boundary walls, in the architecture of several houses (those characterised by a Tuscan-type atrium), in the public buildings in the Triangular Forum and in the Temple of Apollo in the Civic Forum.

Meanwhile Rome had begun its gradual advance towards southern Italy and had started to overcome the resistance of the Italic peoples. As a consequence, even the Samnites were forced to surrender to the Eternal City, though only after three long and bitter wars, the last of which was fought in the years between 298 and 290 B.C. As a result of the conquest of Campania, Pompeii also fell under Roman dominion, becoming an "associate", a status which allowed the maintenance of some degree of local autonomy.

From that time on, its history was closely connected with that of the Eternal City and only on the occasion of the social war waged by the Italic peoples in a final attempt to defend their freedom, did it ally itself with the insurrectionary movement (91 B.C.). In 89 B.C., however, it was besieged by Silla, taken by storm and thus brought back under the aegis of Rome. In 80 B.C. it became a Roman colony with the name of Colonia Cornelia Veneria Pompei.

As in the past, Pompeii continued to expand and develop in every sector, particularly in the economic field, greatly helped by its fertile hinterland and advantageous position. All activities linked to trade and maritime traffic enjoyed a period of growth.

This remarkable development had immediate results: externally, it led to an increase in the level of Pompeii's prestige compared with the other towns of Campania; internally, as a consequence of growing wealth, there was a general increase in the standard of living for many of the social classes. As a result the "middle-class", that is to say the class of merchants and entrepreneurs who had built Pompeii's fortune and had reaped their reward, was able to establish itself in an increasingly prominent way. Pompeii's flourishing economy led to a decisive population increase, widespread affluence and in addition the remarkable embellishment of the town. It is true to say that the middle-class derived great pleasure from competing with the nobility in the construction

of splendid villas. In their desire to outdo the aristocratic class who traditionally held power, the newly rich vied by displaying their own wealth in the opulence of their houses and the preciousness of their ornaments and jewellery. The expansion in urban building took place for the most part along Via dell'Abbondanza, a symbolic centre for the new emerging class.

However, the life and splendour of Pompeii were destined to come to an end. The first inklings of the tragedy were felt in about 62 A.D., when a violent earthquake devastated the city and the surrounding countryside.

It took an immense effort to recover from this blow. The least well-off class suffered the most serious consequences, having seen their houses destroyed. Most of the public and private buildings were still at the stage of being strengthened and restored when Vesuvius became active, and in the space of a few hours

wrought death and destruction on the city. It was 24 August in the year 79 A.D.

A heavy shower of ash, lapilli and lava from the volcano began to rain down onto the city and onto nearby Herculaneum and Stabiae. All was buried beneath a thick blanket of volcanic material to a depth of several metres. The inhabitants, who for the most part fled in the direction of the coast, were suffocated by the fumes of the gases; others met death in their own homes.

Reminders of the past and the fascination of the excavated city

*P*ompeii is one of the most significant examples of the Roman civilization and, like an open book, provides

outstanding information on the art, customs, trades and everyday life of the past. From the darkness of centuries the city has re-emerged precisely as it would have been when it was unexpectedly buried in the thick layer of ash and lava which poured down from the devastating eruption of Vesuvius.

It was the year 79 A.D. The scale of the tragedy was appalling: in what had been one of the most active and splendid Roman centres, life came to a permanent standstill. The thick layer of volcanic material which submerged it, made up to a large extent of ash and lapilli - non-solid material, unlike that which covered Herculaneum and which solidified into extremely hard stone - has meant that the city has remained intact until the present day, not only as far as its buildings are concerned, but also as regards the contents inside the houses and shops, providing an absolutely fascinating picture of "daily" life.

Two representations of the terrible eruption of 79 A.D. exhibited in the Museo Vesuviano in Pompeii. Since then the tragedy that destroyed the city has inspired generations of artists, awed by the inexorable fury of nature.

Opposite: an idyllic scene of the countryside at the foot of Vesuvius in an old painting in the Museo Vesuviano, Pompeii. The smoke emerging from the mouth of the volcano takes on a rather witty aspect.

The walls of the houses are covered with electoral propaganda messages or risqué jokes aimed at particular citizens. The signs on the shop doorways indicate the activity carried out there or the name of the owner. Alongside the elegant villas belonging to the nobility and the luxurious residences of the middle class, stand modest houses where several families lived. The peasant dwellings on the other hand are situated around vegetable gardens or small plots of land. On the edge of the city stood the brothels, squalid rooms intended as places of pleasure for sailors and travellers passing through. In the narrow lanes, the workshops and services provide further evidence of the daily routine performed by workmen and slaves as well as the women of the house.

The houses still contain furniture, ornaments, gold and silverware, work tools, kitchenware, bronze and terracotta lamps, foodstuffs of all kinds, counters for serving drinks, grain mills and grindstones, workshops for manufacturing cloth, smithies and shops selling groceries, fruit and vegetables.

The discoveries made in Pompeii provide a remarkable record of Roman painting, of which virtually nothing would be known otherwise.

The architecture and development of the various types of houses is also amply documented.

Thus the excavated city provides outstanding historical evidence of Roman civilization: these reminders of the past, which are so vivid and tangible in the remains brought to light, contribute to the fascination of the present.

General appearance of the city

P ompeii shows the typical topography of a Roman city with its decuman and cardinal roads (the principal thoroughfares) which intersect at right angles, creating an orthogonal grid: the cardo follows a north-south direction, the decumanus lies east-west.

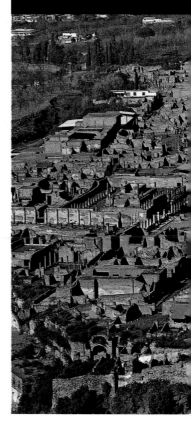

The principal axes consist of Via di Nola (the major decuman road) and Via di Stabia (the main cardinal road).

With the expansion of the city, two other streets were added to support the urban layout and run almost parallel to the former: these are Via dell'Abbondanza, which became the town's new main decuman road, and the Via del Foro, which lay parallel to Via di Stabia to make a second cardinal road. Both were linked to the large civic Forum which constituted the centre of the town's political and economic life.

Two important crossroads - the Orpheus crossroads and the Holconius crossroads - were the junctions for the main axes in Pompeii. Around these axes a close network of streets sprang up, which served to mark off entire blocks of houses (insulae).

The urban centre, with the exception of the Forum area which lies on a flat piece of land, is characterized by a remarkable difference in level caused by the lava terracing which spread across the lower slopes of the mountain.

The layout of the city is rectangular in form.

Around it runs the elliptical perimeter of the walls which extend for about 3 km along the edge of the basalt terracing: several stretches date back to the Samnite era, others to the expansion which

Above, a general view of the archaeological excavations that reveals the extent and the urban complexity that the Roman city had reached. Below, two striking casts of victims of the 79 A.D. eruption, caught forever in the precise moment of their awful death.

took place in the Roman age. Various gates open into the defensive boundary wall: their names are Marina, Ercolano, Vesuvio, Nocera, Capua and Sarno.

The most ancient centre in Pompeii is the part massed around the Triangular Forum. The new Forum, on the other hand, was built in the vicinity of Porta Marina beyond the centre, when the city, which by now had increased remarkably, felt the need for a larger space.

The Theatre, the Amphitheatre and the Gymnasium were built in the peripheral area.

Thermal baths were set up in several parts of the city so that they might answer more adequately the needs of the citizens by serving the various urban areas.

Outside each gate lay a large burial ground with sepulchral monuments.

As evidence of the city's enormous urban expansion, a vast urbanized peripheral area was discovered outside Porta di Ercolano: it contains houses, workshops and superb villas such as that of Diomedes and the Villa of the Mysteries. Another of the suburban villas which characterized the period of greatest expansion of Pompeii is located in the vicinity of Porta Marina, and is known as the suburban villa of Porta Marina.

The houses can be dated back to various historical periods: those belonging to the pre-Samnite period are simpler in their layout and almost always made of tufa stone; those of the Samnite period are more elaborate; without doubt those from the Roman age show the greatest degree of perfection.

The temples in Pompeii are concentrated in the area of the large Forum and the Triangular Forum and reproduce traditional Greek designs.

Plenty examples of workshops can be found throughout the city: there are numerous fullonicae (places for the treatment of cloth), a fundamental sector in Pompeii's economy, to the extent that the Dyers' Guild had its own building in the Forum (named the Building of Eumachia) containing shops and warehouses for the storage of goods.

There are a good many thermopolia, which were refreshment rooms (the equivalent of modern-day bars), intended for the serving of drinks and recognizable from the counters with holes in them used to hold amphora. In addition we find bakeries and mills, often attached to warehouses for storing grain. In general, all the workshops are adjacent to the house of their owner, thus making it more convenient for him to do his job and allowing him to involve his entire family and servants in the enterprise as well.

Pompeii had a supply of hotels and rooms to let: several buildings bear inscriptions which are advertisements for leases.

Private baths were also frequently let out. Furthermore there were plenty of gambling dens and houses of pleasure (lupanari).

Among the curiosities worthy of note are the pedestrian crossings located at the road junctions: these consist of very large stones placed crosswise along the streets: people were able to walk on these and so avoid getting their feet wet in case of rain. It is interesting to observe the signs on the shops, often in the form of painted pictures and depicting the activity carried out there and the name of the owner.

The walls of the houses are dotted with inscriptions: these are public announcements of performances or advertisements for rooms to let, as well as electoral propaganda messages and words of a lewd nature referring to various people or situations.

General lay-out of the city

The House

There is ample documentation of the Roman house in Pompeii, from modest dwellings to large and magnificent villas with sumptuous decorations, from simple workmen's houses to the elegant residences of the nobility, from the homes of merchants which were built around their workshops, to those with their own vegetable garden and plots of land used for agricultural purposes.

The typical house is variable in size and has a rectangular plan. It is almost totally devoid of windows on the outside, since all the rooms face onto the inner courtyards.

A typical house of the first period was formed by a "Tuscan" atrium: the

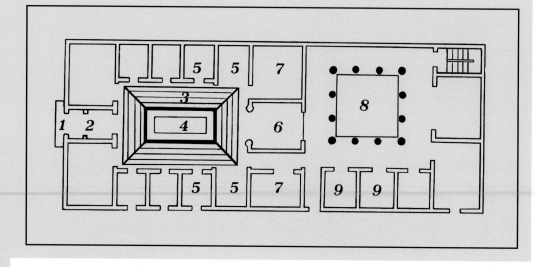

1 - *Vestibulum* or entrance-way.
2 - *Fauces* or entrance passage.
3 - Atrium or forecourt.
4 - *Impluvium* or cistern into which the rainwater drained from the roof.
5 - *Cubicula*; these generally formed the living quarters of members of the family.
6 - *Tablinium* which assumed varying functions according to period, sometimes serving as a bedroom or a living room.
7 - *Alae* or wings.
8 - *Peristylium*, the latter was represented in the first period simply by a garden.
9 - *Triclinium*, which became the new dining room.

entrance or vestibulum, *often closed off by a wooden door, gave access to the atrium. This was covered by a sloping roof* (compluvium) *open in such a way as to channel rainwater into the* impluvium.

In subsequent periods it was known as tetrastyle, because it was embellished with four columns which supported the impluvium. Around this room ran a colonnade and a series of rooms known as cubicula, *which*

were the family's sleeping quarters.

The atrium was followed by the tablinium *(meeting and reception room) and the* triclinium *or dining room. The garden opened onto the back of the house and was surrounded by a colonnade or* peristylium. *The latter, adopted from Hellenistic models, was the result of the transformation of the old kitchen garden (several villas had a garden as well as a vegetable patch) and led to the expansion of the residence and to the creation of rooms used for receiving guests* (oecus). *At the back of the house were the kitchens and storehouses. With the passing of time the house greatly increases in terms of size, the spaces and rooms being doubled, to the point that it occupies almost an entire* insula. *At the same time it becomes particularly*

Ideal reconstruction of a luxurious Roman house.

refined and pays special attention to embellishments and elegant decorations. With the gradual development of the middle-class, the model house saw further modifications dictated by the new needs of the resident families. First and foremost, workshops were added in which the owner could carry out his activity. The apartment lay at the back of these and above and, in most houses, is linked to the rest by staircases and accessways.

In this case the house shows a more simplified plan, since part of the space was taken up by the workshops.

The Temples

Roman temples - the ones in Pompeii in particular - do not diverge in any way from the great Hellenistic models known through the colonies of Magna Graecia.

The main nucleus was provided by a cella (naos) - where the statue of the god was housed - enclosed in a larger structure usually rectangular in shape.

The latter varied in its

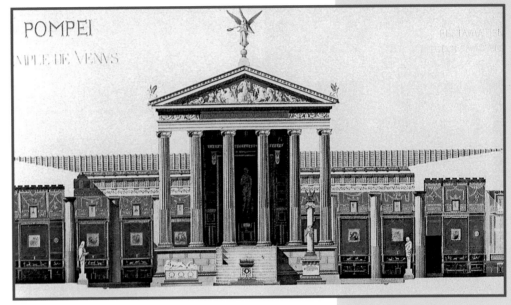

structure according to the arrangement of the colonnade: the temple with columns incorporated in the central front part was called in antis; a temple the whole front of which opened onto a colonnade was known as prostyle; one with columns placed at front and back was called amphiprostyle; the temple with a ring of columns around its entire perimeter was peripteral and that whose perimeter was surrounded by a double colonnade was dipteral. The shape of the capitals gave

rise to a further distinction in three orders: Doric, Ionic and Corinthian according to whether they were completely flattened, had two side volutes or were decorated with acanthus leaves.

Thermal Baths

The thermae were the city's public baths. There were relatively few private baths and these were limited to the most wealthy families, given that the latter were the

Above, a 19th-century reconstruction of the Temple of Venus in Pompeii. Below, a view of the Stabian Baths.

only ones who could afford to build rooms suited to the purpose.

The thermal bath buildings were divided into two sections: one reserved for women and one reserved for men. Each of these contained a series of rooms with different functions: 1) apodyterium or changing room

Above, a view of the Grand Theatre.
Right, one of the exquisite friezes that decorate the House of Vettii.

2) frigidarium *or cold bath room*
3) tepidarium *or tepid bath room*
4) calidarium *or hot bath room.*
The thermal baths included latrines and, in the most developed type, a pool and gymnasium. They were often furnished with open spaces and gardens.
The system of heating the rooms - which was fairly ingenious - worked by running heated water through the cavities in the wall.
The thermae *were not only buildings used as a public utility, but also played a very important social role in that they provided an important place for people to meet.*

Theatre

*T*he theatre was the place where performances of comedies and tragedies were held.
It included a semi-circular cavea *from which led the series of steps divided into sections on which the spectators sat.*
Below was the area for the orchestra *(the part intended for the chorus) and the* scena, *that is the stage where the actors performed.*
The theatre in Pompeii shows the features of Greek models in that it exploits the natural inclination of the terrain. The Roman-type theatre on the other hand depends on an architectural structure.

Amphitheatre

*I*t is presumed that the amphitheatre in Pompeii, the oldest known to us, must have provided the basic model for the subsequent buildings.
The form derives from the duplication of the structure of the theatre (amphitheatre means "double theatre" or "circular theatre"): it is an elliptical structure situated in a depression in the ground and backing onto embankments.
It consists of a large cavea around which are the steps, divided into sections, which cover the entire perimeter of the construction. The various sections of the cavea - ima cavea *(low part),* media cavea, *(middle part) and* summa cavea *(upper part) - were intended for the various social classes: the seats in the lower central area were reserved for dignitaries, while those high up were for the plebeians. It was furnished with accessways to the seats as well as with entrances to the* cavea. *The amphitheatres were sometimes equipped with a* velarium *(a large canopy which was stretched over the amphitheatre in case of rain) and, in the more developed types, with a system of canals and bulkheads which allowed the* cavea *to be flooded so that naval battles could be staged.*

Painting

*B*efore the discovery of Pompeii, information about Roman painting was scarce and fragmentary with rare examples limited to fragments of frescoes found in isolated cases. The discovery of the city, with its rich pictorial heritage, has, however, allowed for a new debate to be opened on the whole issue of Roman art. On the basis of the studies carried out and the classification made by Vitruvius, the paintings are usually divided into 4 styles:
I style: known as "incrustation" or "structural" style. It was commonplace between the 2nd century and the middle of the 1st century B.C. It is a simple and bare style of painting: through the use of plaster and colours in which black, yellow and red predominate, it tends to imitate marble panels.
II style: in use until the middle of the 1st century A.D. It is known as architecture in perspective or simply architectural since, as well as faking marble facings, it reproduces colonnades, arches and buildings seen in perspective. The result is an imaginary space with increasing or decreasing effects. The great cycle of the Mysteries in the villa of the same name belongs to this period. At its most advanced stage, glimpses of the countryside are painted between the imaginary buildings.
III style: called "real painting" this belongs to the 1st century A.D. It sees a return to a simpler style in terms of the layout and stroke. The background becomes flat and is rendered with a single colour: the figures are embellished and the decorative elements accentuated. The painting of the III style is also known as "Egyptian" or "Ornamental" in that the ornamentation often recalls ancient Egyptian motifs.
IV style: is known as "architectural illusionism" or "ornamental". Its characteristics recall the painting of the second period, but the composition becomes increasingly exaggerated and unreal. It almost seems as if there was an attempt to extend the walls through the

creation of imaginary spaces. The decoration becomes, so to speak, quasi-baroque: the houses are filled with stuccos and overloaded with ornamentation, usually in demonstration of the opulent state achieved by the resident families. Friezes and festoons are abandoned.

Mosaics

*M*osaic ornamentation was widely used in the decoration of the houses in Pompeii and saw various stages of development. The oldest examples are works executed with simple motifs, using tesserae of rough workmanship and of modest material; those of subsequent epochs, on the other hand, show refinement in their composition, taste in colour, and in the preciousness of the tesserae used. In the first period the works are characterized by the repetition of simple geometric motifs or they

repeat the pictorial patterns of the second, third and fourth phases. Mosaics were often used as flooring. There are some admirable examples: the famous "cave canem" placed at the entrance to many houses is perhaps the best-known among the many which have survived. The panel depicting "The Battle of Issos" housed in the Archaeological Museum in Naples and originating from the House of the Faun, is, though, one of the most important and magnificent examples.

Sculpture

*T*he sculptures which have survived show that in Pompeii there was a preference for statues of a small size, given that they were designed for ornamental purposes, to be incorporated into rooms and gardens, to embellish fountains, atriums or tablinia. The large statues, those which had a commemorative function, were

for the most part situated in the Forum. The favoured material was bronze, although there are plenty of small masterpieces in marble, tufa stone and terracotta. "The Dancing Faun", the "Drunken Silenus" and the "Wild boar under attack" are just some of the pieces which combine exquisite workmanship with the freshness and immediacy of their design. A special mention should be given to the "Doryphorus", a beautiful copy of a splendid Greek sculpture. There are various fragments of statues

originating for the most part from the area of the Forum and from the temples dedicated to the Capitoline Triad.

Inscriptions and graffiti

*T*he walls of the houses in Pompeii are frequently covered with inscriptions: these are electoral propaganda messages which urge the citizens to vote for one or other of the candidates.
At times an entire category of

workers (goldsmiths, marble-cutters, bakers, blacksmiths) holds the candidacy. At other times an aspiring magistrate puts himself forward to the people for a particular office.

They are written in red or in black and for the most part in capital letters. They were executed by the professional scribes who also dealt with official communications, the sentences of the tribunal, the buying and selling of slaves and public decisions. There are around three thousand electoral inscriptions in Pompeii and most of them can be dated to the city's final year of existence, given that it was customary to rub out the old inscriptions to make way for new ones. The graffiti, on the other hand, are the messages which were made by scratching on the walls of the houses: these relate to the most disparate subjects and paint an extremely vivid and frank picture of contemporary social life: they include risqué jokes, comments on a particular person or event, caricatures of famous people, reflections on love, as well as appreciative remarks about a beautiful woman or the pleasure experienced in the privacy of one of the rooms in the brothel. In addition there are several which are concerned with the buying and selling of materials or livestock and the calculation of merchandise. Many refer to the entertainments on offer in the city or are in praise of the champions put to the test in the gladiatorial games.

Three renowned images of ancient Pompeii: left, the copy of the Dancing Faun, a little masterpiece in bronze found in the house now named after him, where the splendid mosaic portraying a tragic mask (above opposite), was also discovered. Opposite page, below, one of the many engraved stones that are seen on the walls of the city.

A visitor arriving to explore the archaeological excavations of Pompeii today first reaches what was one of the seven gates in the defensive walls of the ancient city, Porta Marina which was one of the most impressive but, given the difficult and sloping road that led to it, was certainly not the most used gate. The walls, already in existence in the 6th century B.C., had a rampart walk, and were protected externally by a ditch and internally by an embankment. They were over three kilometres in length and had twelve towers, more numerous on the northern side where the land was flatter and therefore more difficult to defend. Within the walls life pulsated in this busy, lively city.

1 PORTA MARINA

This is the main entrance to the excavations of Pompeii and takes its name from its seaward-facing position. It stands on the western side of the boundary wall. At one time it bore the name of Porta Neptunia and, notwithstanding its vicinity to the area of the Forum, was never the preferred access of the Pompeians, given that it opened onto a stretch of very steep and uneven terrain, making it somewhat inconvenient. The gate consists of two arches with barrel vaults: one, the more awkward, was used for the transit of beasts of burden, the other for pedestrians.

2 THE SUBURBAN BATHS

Recently restored with particular attention to the splendid frescoes in the *apodyterium* (changing rooms) the Suburban Baths are located immediately outside the Porta Marina on the north. Built against the city walls, on an artificial terrace facing towards the sea, they are unusual in that they consist of a single structure and are not divided into male and female (1st century B.C. – 1st century A.D.). Splendid decorations enhanced the thermal baths themselves: a hot covered pool, a smaller cold pool and a pretty waterfall situated inside an artificial grotto made of mosaic. Painted walls and stucco work were found throughout but, as mentioned, the decoration in the changing rooms is quite outstanding with sixteen paintings showing erotic scenes and positions, including between two women, the only of its kind in Roman painting.
Seriously damaged by the earthquake of 62 A.D, the baths must have been rebuilt and at the same time newly decorated. With the eruption that buried Pompeii they fell into oblivion until finally they were rediscovered as late as the 1950s. Thus an entire complex has come to light that provides valuable information regarding everyday life in a city of the 1st century A.D.

A landscape fresco inside the House of Marcus Lucretius which, with its splendid reproductions of houses, helps us to envisage how the Roman city of Pompeii appeared before the eruption of 79 A.D.

THE FORUM

This was the ideal centre of the city, providing a religious nucleus (the main temples stood here, such as those dedicated to Jupiter, father of all the gods, Apollo and the Lares) and a political axis, in that it was here that justice was administered and the town's public institutions were situated. In addition it was the economic heart of the city, the place where bargaining and commercial transactions took place. It was also the site of the storehouses for foodstuffs and, in some cases, of the headquarters for the most representative categories of workers. The Forum was a vast square usually situated in a central position. The one in Pompeii, which consists of a large rectangular area with a perimeter of more than 400 metres, is situated in the south-western section and therefore decentralized compared to the inhabited centre. The choice of location was determined, among other factors, by the need to find an area that was extensive and level enough, which given Pompeii's situation on lava terracing was no mean feat. In the subsequent period, the Civic Forum grew up on the site of the older and more central Triangular Forum, although there were plenty of buildings

in the area dating back to the Samnite epoch, such as the Temple of Apollo. This happened when, owing to changing socio-economic conditions, the marked population increase and constant urban expansion, it became necessary to create a new public space which could more adequately fulfil the changing needs of the population and the dignity of the city itself. As a consequence, the area which until the 2nd century B.C. had been set aside for the town market, was now utilized. The Forum in Pompeii stands at the junction of the town's main roads, the Via dell'Abbondanza in particular, which was the most important centre of the prosperous Roman city. The remains of this important social meeting place show only in part the majesty and the beauty that previously existed. The image which the Forum once projected was undoubtedly far more magnificent and monumental: it is enough to consider that the square used to be surrounded on three sides by a long and elegant colonnade which in its turn was surmounted by an airy open gallery. Between the columns stood statues of illustrious personages as well as the dais set aside for orators. At the far end rose the flight of steps of the Capitolium or Temple of Jupiter which spectacularly closed off the fourth side of the square.

GENERAL LOCATION PLAN OF THE FORUM

1 - Temple of Jupiter

2 - Arch of Nero

3 - Macellum (market)

4 - Sanctuary of the Lares

5 - Temple of Vespasian

6 - Basilica

7 - Temple of Apollo

8 - Warehouses

9 - Latrines

10 - City treasury

11 - Commemorative arch

12 - Forum baths

13 - Temple of Fortuna Augusta

14 - Arch of Caligula

15 - Via dell'Abbondanza

16 - Workshops

17 - Eumachia Building

18 - Comitium

19 - Office of the *aediles*

20 - Curia

21 - Office of the *duoviri*

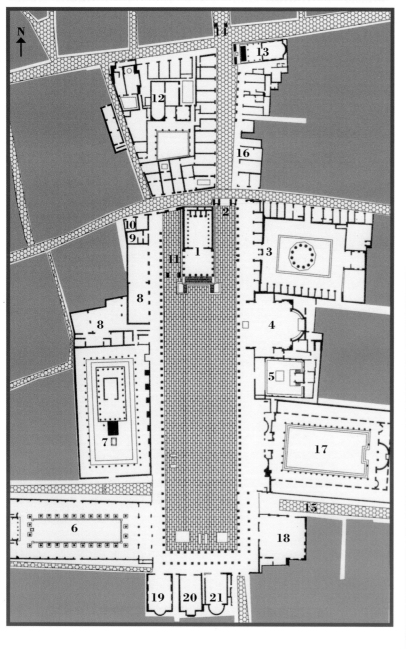

3 THE COLONNADE

It runs round three sides of the Forum (the fourth, the north side, is occupied by the Temple of Jupiter). The oldest part is on the southern side: it was executed in the Samnite epoch and the material used was tufa stone. The colonnade and the trabeation of the western and eastern sections on the other hand are made of travertine marble and may be attributed to the Roman age. The open gallery which ran above the arcade was formed by soaring columns: part of it can still be made out on the western side. Between the columns of the colonnade were numerous sculptures dedicated to illustrious personages: today only some of their pedestals remain.

The Buildings in the Forum

4 TEMPLE OF APOLLO

This temple is an integral part of the Forum area even though it predates it. It dates back, at least as far as its primitive nucleus is concerned, to the 6th century, that is during the Samnite period. It was then extended, particularly under the Emperor Nero, and the part which jutted out into the Forum square was closed off and embellished around the 1st century A.D.
The building shows architectural features of both Italic and Greek derivation and has a rectangular plan with the perimeter being surrounded by an astonishing 48 columns. The inner cella, raised on a podium, was reached by means of a long flight of steps. Opposite these was the sacrificial altar.
The central part, which contains the altar to the god, is also surrounded by columns. It is adorned with two statues depicting "Apollo shooting arrows" and "Diana" (the originals are housed in the National Archaeological Museum in Naples). On one of the columns which mark off the cella of the god there was a sun dial.

PLAN

1 - Entrance
2 - Colonnaded portico
3 - Portico with niches
4 - Podium
5 - Cella with the divinity
6 - Altar

The statues of "Apollo shooting arrows" (left and above) and "Diana", copies of the original bronzes now in the National Archaeological Museum in Naples, still reign proudly amidst the impressive ruins of the Temple of Apollo.

THE SUN DIAL

A small sun dial can still be seen on the one surviving column of the many that originally surrounded the cella in the Temple of Apollo. Apollo was, in fact, also venerated as the sun god and both this and a similar sun dial in the Triangular Forum were generously donated to the city by the *duoviri* L. Sepunius and M. Eremius. It is still clear from the inscriptions that these two most eminent magistrates of Pompeii were proud of having given these simple sundials to the citizens and indeed this is not surprising, for even in ancient times the possibility of measuring the passing of time was considered a most necessary prerequisite for the smooth running of a thriving civil and social life.

5 BASILICA

A magnificent building, monumental in its proportions and importance, it represented the nucleus of the Forum as it was here that the public life of the town was centred. The construction is preceded by a colonnade and consists of a large rectangular room divided lengthwise by a series of columns (28 altogether) into three naves. A row of demi-columns stands against the walls. At the back of the building was the raised area set aside for the tribunal, distinguished by two orders of columns placed in front. Access was gained to it by two flights of stairs.

The parts still visible today bear witness to the elegance and the balanced architectural design of the complex. The Basilica was probably executed around the 2nd century B.C. (this can be inferred from the inscriptions and several factory marks imprinted on the tiles). Some experts, on the basis of the discovery of several tiles and on the study of the position of the columns, have speculated that the building may have been covered by a roof, whilst others maintain that the central nave must have been trabeated and open to the sky.

The Basilica in ancient Rome was the place set aside for the administration of justice (Tribunal) as well as being the building where contracts of various kinds were stipulated and legalized. In the more ancient temples, at the dawning of Greek civilization, it was the seat of the king (in Greek "basileus" meant "king") and therefore the place which symbolized the highest level of power. When, as a result of changing political conditions, it ceased to be the seat of a sovereign, it became the place set aside for the administration of judicial power, continuing to play a role of the greatest importance throughout the imperial age. With the fall of the empire and after the arrival of Christianity, the building, with all its architectural features and together with the name which distinguishes it, became the place where religious functions were performed: all the Catholic, and in particular the early Christian churches, were called "basilicas" as a result and had the same plan and structure as the Roman model.

PLAN

1 - Main entrance
    (chalcidicum)
2 - Portico
3 - Central hall
4 - Tribunal

of archaeological material found in Pompeii and are therefore filled with all manner of items from amphora to tufa sculptures, marble decorations to pediments, from relief carvings to the remains of what were once trees or men, as some casts of victims of the eruption are also housed here.

It is really quite difficult for someone entering the ancient Forum Olitorium today to imagine how it might have once looked as a busy fruit and vegetable market with shops and stores overflowing with the freshest of produce. Currently, in fact, the premises are used as storage for the most disparate kinds

6 THE HORREA AND FORUM OLITORIUM

Also known as the "Forum Granary", the section along the western side of the Forum with eight large brick pilasters on the façade housed a large market where the cereals, herbs, fruit and vegetables produced by the fertile soil of the area, were sold. There were also spacious warehouses where the goods were stored as well as two rooms that probably served as the State Treasury or *Aerarium*. Built after the earthquake of 62 A.D., the Forum Granary is not decorated inside, possibly because the construction was not entirely completed at the time of the disastrous eruption.

7 THE MENSA PONDERARIA

Not far from the market, along the east wall of the Temple of Apollo, was the *Mensa Ponderaria*, a complete public weights and measures office created in the 2nd century

FOOD AND DRINK IN POMPEII

Meals in Pompeii usually consisted of the delicious produce that the fertile volcanic terrain at the foot of Vesuvius and the generous Mediterranean sea provided in abundance. Thus bread, cheese and vegetables were usually eaten at breakfast, and this was followed by a light lunch of fried fish, salsiccia, focaccia, fruit and occasionally a sweet. But the main meal of the day was supper which could be prepared from 4 o'clock in the afternoon onwards. This consisted of appetizers, meat, fish, vegetables and abundant fresh fruit with a choice of desserts to finish. Indeed food was considered to be highly important in Pompeii as is evident from the large number of taverns, trattorias and food shops in the city. Food products from Pompeii were in fact particularly well-known and in demand in the ancient world, such as Pompeian bread and the famous *Vesuvinum*, made with local grapes and exported to Gaul, Britain and Spain, but the unique *garum* in particular represented the high point of Pompeian gastronomy. This sauce made from the innards of various fish was strained through wicker baskets, collected in jars and preserved in salt to then be exported in great quantities. With a unique flavour, it was combined with wine, vinegar or herbs to make a condiment for a great variety of dishes.

B.C. to protect citizens from the possible vagaries of merchants. The legal control of measures of weight and volume was carried out here and was originally based on the Oscan system of measurements which was only replaced by the Roman system established by Augustus in 20 B.C. Two limestone benches were used for the purpose, containing nine hollows that corresponded to the various measures; once the goods were weighed, they were released through a hole in the bottom of the cavity.

Everyday objects from Pompeii: jugs, a bronze pot with an artistically decorated handle and, alongside, scales with a counterweight in the form of a human head.

8 TEMPLE OF JUPITER OR CAPITOLIUM

This was the main centre of religious life in Pompeii. Situated on the northern side of the Forum, it is dedicated to the highest divinity of ancient times - it was in fact built in honour of the Jupter, Juno and Minerva triad - and towers above a broad staircase with two large arches on either side which have remained virtually intact; it closed off the fourth side of the square where there was no colonnade, in a quite spectacular manner.

The temple, dating back to the 2nd century B.C., was built in two stages, the second of which, scheduled towards the end of the same century, led to the extension of the architectural structure. The building shows at the front the remains of some tall fluted columns: these also continued along the sides as far as the cella which is spacious and fairly elongated.
The large "head of Jupiter" found here is in the Archaeological Museum in Naples. The building was seriously damaged by the earthquake of 62 A.D. and, at the moment of the eruption of 79 A.D., it had not yet been restored to its original splendour.

Right, a splendid view of the remains of the Temple of Capitoline Jupiter, flanked by two commemorative arches behind which – imperious and unmistakable – rises the outline of Vesuvius.

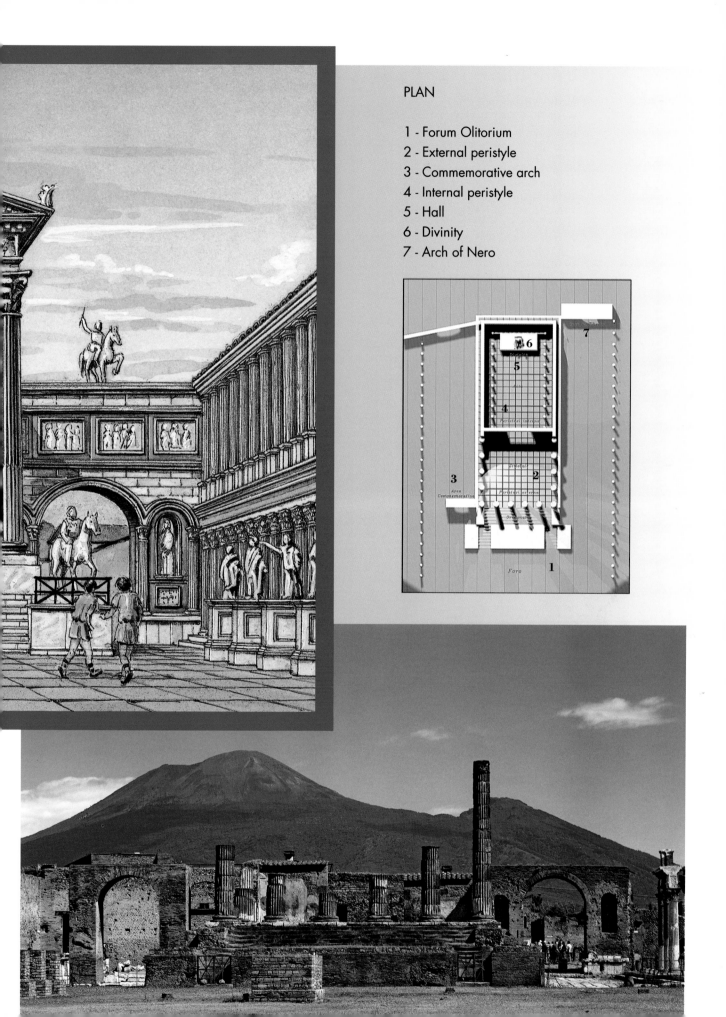

PLAN

1 - Forum Olitorium
2 - External peristyle
3 - Commemorative arch
4 - Internal peristyle
5 - Hall
6 - Divinity
7 - Arch of Nero

9 MEMORIAL ARCHES

The Forum was the most important public area in the city and in the northern section, flanking the Temple of Jupiter, stood a series of imposing honorary arches made of brick (but probably covered with marble) the purpose of which was to celebrate the glories of the imperial family. Thus the arch standing to the north-west (facing page, above right and below) commemorates Augustus while its twin to the east of the temple façade no longer exists though it is thought that it was dedicated to Nero and was destroyed after his death due to his reprehensible behaviour. On its removal however, the arch behind (this page, below right and right), further to the north, gained in significance; on one side are two niches that probably housed statues of Nero and Drusus while on the other were two fountains. In ancient times it was probably crowned by an equestrian statue, probably portraying Tiberius. Still further north, at the beginning of Via di Mercurio where there is a crossroads, rises another arch which is associated with Caligula (facing page, above left), perhaps simply because an equestrian statue believed to represent this emperor was found nearby and could originally have been located over the arch.

The inscription on the arch reads:

IN HONORE
CALIGULAE
HIC ARCUS

MEMORIA EORUM QUI REI
PUBLICAE PROFUERUNT
SEMPITERNA ERIT

TRIUMPHUS
ERECTUS EST
ANNO XXC

10 THE MACELLUM

This was the name of the city market, recently restored. It dates back to the 1st century A.D., is square in shape and was preceded by a wide colonnade beneath which were the entrances to shops.

The *Macellum* had three entrances, one of which, the main one, was furnished with an aedicule. Inside the building were more *tabernae* (shops), while in the centre was an aedicule with a dome, supported by twelve columns, that covered a tank full of water.

This was probably the part used for the fish market, a theory supported by the discovery of fragments of fish bones in the drainage canal.

Of particular interest is what remains of a marvellous painting which adorned the back wall of the building.

Some of the numerous statues which originally embellished the construction have also been found in the macellum.

11 TEMPLE OF THE LARES

This sanctuary was dedicated to the protector gods of the house and was built by the Pompeians as a token of their gratitude for having escaped the perilous earthquake. Executed in brick, it has a rectangular plan enlivened at the far end by an apse with fine ornamental columns and with niches either side.

Views of the Macellum, with a glimpse of the remains of the portico that surrounded the area of the Forum (above right), and two of the numerous statues which originally embellished the construction (above).

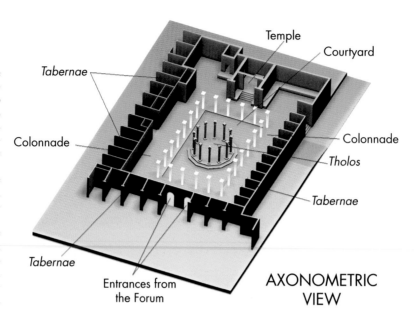

Temple

Courtyard

Tabernae

Colonnade

Colonnade

Tholos

Tabernae

Tabernae

Entrances from the Forum

AXONOMETRIC VIEW

The Lares were the tutelary deities of the house and were probably to be identified with the deceased: they protected the property and the family. Each house had a site or a small temple dedicated to them.

12 TEMPLE OF VESPASIAN

This is a small cult building of which part of the façade of the outer structure still remains - the side walls are decorated with blind gabled windows - and a cella raised on a pedestal. The latter, standing on a podium, was at one time preceded by four fluted columns supporting a pediment. Opposite is an altar in marble decorated with bas-reliefs depicting "sacrificial scenes".

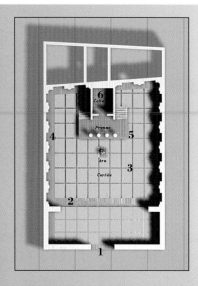

PLAN

1 - Entrance from the Forum
2 - Internal courtyard
3 - Altar
4 - Niches
5 - Pronaos
6 - Cella

13 THE EUMACHIA BUILDING

Built during the reign of the Emperor Tiberius, it was commissioned by the priestess Eumachia to accommodate the guild of *fullones* or launderers and dyers of cloth, a category whose importance was such that it could afford to have its principal headquarters in the economic and social heart of the city. In terms of its proportions

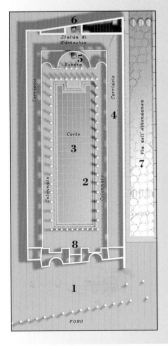

PLAN

1 - Forum Olitorium
2 - Colonnade
3 - Internal courtyard
4 - *Cryptoporticus* (corridor)
5 - Exedra
6 - Statue of Eumachia
7 - Via dell'Abbondanza
8 - Entrance from the Forum

this building is inferior only to the Basilica. At the front is a colonnade above which unfurls a dedicatory inscription to the priestess. Worthy of note is the magnificent portal characterized by an elegant decoration of acanthus leaves. Inside was a spacious colonnade which followed the perimeter of the courtyard and which ended at the back in three apses, one of which housed the statue of *Concordia* personified in the figure of Livia, wife of the Emperor Augustus.

At the back, on the other hand, was a corridor, or *cryptoporticus*, probably used for the storage of cloth which was then sold in the open space of the courtyard. It was here that the statue dedicated to Eumachia stood.

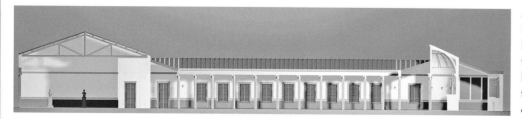

A reconstruction of the Eumachia Building; this longitudinal section emphasizes the magnificence and the harmonious architectural design that characterized this imposing construction.

14 MUNICIPAL OFFICES

These three buildings occupy the southern side of the Forum. Each was used for dealing with the paperwork and the services related to the ranks of the *duoviri*, the *aediles* and the *decurioni*. The buildings are virtually identical. The central one was probably the Archive and was furnished with shelves, as can be inferred from the space created by the pillars which demarcate the inner walls.

The *duoviri*: the most important office in the city. They fulfilled a role similar to that of the consuls and had a mainly judicial function.

The *decurioni* were the representatives of the town senate.

The *aediles* supervised the running of public services.

15 THE COMITIUM

This public area was subdivided into various sectors and was used to carry out all electoral procedures. Voting in the elections for the magistrates of Pompeii was held here. All free male citizens were entitled to vote in Pompeii and they cast their vote in the section of the Comitium that corresponded to the district in which they resided and which formed a genuine constituency. The vote was made in writing and the counting of the votes also took place in the Comitium. The candidate with the greatest number of votes in all the constituencies was the elected winner.

THE CENTRE OF POMPEII - ROADS, HOUSES AND SHOPS

16 VIA DELL'ABBONDANZA

Although it was built at a later date than the other thoroughfares in the town, Via dell'Abbondanza soon came to constitute the main road of the city, the street where the new emerging class developed the commercial activities which were to make Pompeii one of the most important centres in Campania. The town's new prestige was at the root of the great changes which took place within Pompeian society and provided, in particular, the opportunity for considerable urban development.

The growing needs of the population were a highly significant factor in this evolution, but also important was the wish of the emerging wealthy class to build houses suited to its new social status, thereby seeking to equal, and even to better in terms of luxury and size, the villas of the nobility.

Along the Via dell'Abbondanza numerous workshops sprang up and, adjoining these, the houses of their owners.

The design of these houses follows different criteria to those of the more classical house. In fact they consist of a series of rooms ranged over at least two floors so that commercial activity could be carried out on the ground floor, with the upper floor being set aside for family life. The two were closely linked, however, and all members of the household were able to fulfil the essential tasks of their trade in the most efficient way possible.

The houses in this area are often furnished with jutting roofs, terraces and entrances.

Via dell'Abbondanza is one of the principal decuman roads of the city: at one end lies the area of the civic Forum and at the other the area of the Amphitheatre, crossing Pompeii in a south-west, north-east direction. Its name is derived from the sign placed on the Fountain of the Holconius Crossroads which depicts a cornucopia, the symbol of plenty or abundance.

Houses and shops were tightly packed along Via dell'Abbondanza, in the centre of the town. Note in particular, below, the pedestrian crossings.
Facing page, pictures of the head with cornucopia of the Fountain of Abundance, which gave its name to the main street of Pompeii.

THE SHOPS OF VIA DELL'ABBONDANZA

Between 1911 and 1912 excavations were begun in Pompeii that were intended to bring to light a long stretch of Via dell'Abbondanza and the buildings facing on to it leading towards the Sarno Gate. These excavations and the subsequent attentive restoration have provided a very lively image of everyday life in what was one of the city's main thoroughfares, with shops and signs to attract customers, two-storey buildings with balconies over the street, electoral posters and propaganda written on the walls as well as graffiti left by passers-by. It would seem that in the years following the earthquake of 62 A.D. Via dell'Abbondanza was becoming the centre of economic activity in Pompeii, particularly in the area around the crossroads with Via Stabiana. Shops in particular were being re-built or newly constructed,

though when the eruption occurred in 79 A.D. it seems that the residential houses had not yet been restored. This was the situation at the only bakery in the street, belonging to Sotericus and built after 72 A.D. by modifying two ruined houses. Alongside was a *caupona* (hostelry), also owned by Sotericus and originally identified with a sign painted with a figure of Rome – *Virtus elmata*, where the obscene graffiti left by the clients describe the sexual pleasures offered by the waitresses and the hostess. Other hostelries stood along Via dell'Abbondanza as well as shops where all kinds of services were provided: laundries, dyers, cloth workers and blacksmiths' workshops like the one which belonged to a certain Verus where a *groma* was found – an instrument used by surveyors to measure lots of land. In the part of the street nearest to the Sarno Gate, and therefore on the edge of the city, the shops became fewer and the houses, such as the house of Octavius Quartio and villa of Julia Felix, assume traditional designs and proportions that are closer to those of suburban villas than to town houses.

17 HOUSE OF THE WILD BOAR

This house contains the remains of some very interesting mosaics. Particularly fine is the one located on the floor of the atrium which gives the house its name and depicts a hunting scene showing a "wild boar assailed by dogs". There is also an exquisite mosaic decoration composed of geometric motifs. The marble floors and the area around the garden are of great beauty.

House of the Wild Boar: a detail of the famous mosaic.

BROTHEL (Lupanare)

The word "lupanare" was used to indicate the houses of pleasure of which there were many in Pompeii.

The name derives from "lupa", the term used to define a woman who would call out to the men below and lure them upstairs to where she was waiting. In general they were small structures, of a very basic kind often consisting of a room above a shop. Only the *lupanare* of the 7th Regio had been built specifically for this purpose at a crossroads - the traditional spot for exercising this particular business.

The building is on two floors with five small, bare rooms on each and including a waiting room, balcony and latrine. The beds in the *cubicula* were made of a stone and were covered with mattresses. The walls were covered with a series of paintings, frescoes and scenes showing amorous embraces, as well as the various services offered by the prostitutes with the relevant price. It offers a realistic image of the social life of the time and completes the picture of a city in its many guises. The girls who worked in the *lupanare* were usually slaves, often Greek or from the east, and they were managed by a *lenone* who ran the brothel.

Sometimes however, these women succeeded in becoming quite famous through their work and thus gained a degree of importance, for it would seem that some of the electoral slogans still legible on the walls of the buildings, indicate the support of one of them for a given candidate as a point in his favour.

18 HOUSE OF THE HANGING BALCONY

This house stands in the lane that is named after it. It is a truly delightful dwelling and especially interesting for the balcony which adorns the façade. The terrace is a recurrent feature in the architecture of Pompeii and is widely found in the area of the new excavations.

19 HOUSE OF THE WOUNDED BEAR

A mosaic in the entrance hall represents a wounded bear, which is trying to pull out from its side the lance which has struck it. Note the beautiful mosaic fountain at the bottom of the garden.

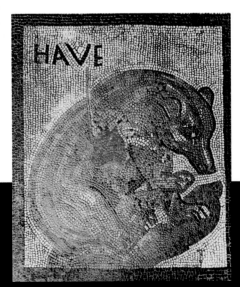

20 THE BAKERY OF POPIDIUS PRISCUS

The shop has all the normal characteristics of bakeries of this time: firstly the stones for milling the grain (four and one smaller one), stores for the flour and the wood-fired oven. However, there is no counter for selling the bread and it is possible that this bakery, which was run by a freedman, only sold its produce as wholesale or made used of travelling sellers (known as *libarii*).

21 HOUSE OF ARIADNE

This is one of the oldest houses in Pompeii. Still visible inside are some fine painted capitals - consequently the dwelling also bears the name of House of the Coloured Capitals - as well as various other paintings executed in the Roman period and belonging to the IV style.

In Pompeii bakeries seem to have been a veritable institution as some 34 have been identified. The use of bread had only become popular among the Romans in the 2nd century and this new product eventually substituted a kind of thick wheat cream also made from the flour and widely used until then.

Bread had an immediate success but the great number of bakeries in Pompeii cannot be explained simply by local use and clearly supports the theory that the famous bread of Pompeii was intended for export at least to the surrounding area, but probably also further afield.

Every bakery had a wood-fired oven and some grinding stones consisting of a conical shaped block (*meta*), fixed on a base and a rotating part shaped like an hourglass (*catillus*) both made from a hard lava stone which does not splinter thus avoiding the risk of small pieces getting into the flour. A shaft operated by slaves or oxen worked the millstones and the rubbing of the two blocks crushed the grain which passed through the *catillus* thus producing the flour. This was then mixed and kneaded turning the paste thus obtained into the most suitable or popular shape. Usually these were in the form of loaves or rings which were then baked in wood-fired ovens.

Incredible as it may seem, many loaves which must have been produced immediately before the eruption of Vesuvius, almost all round shaped and marked into eight segments, were discovered quite carbonized and can now be seen in the Museum of Pompeii.

22 HOUSE OF THE CLASSICAL HUNT

This noble house with its severe design was constructed in the Samnite period as is evident from the architectural style in general, and especially in the choice of materials, such as the tufa stone of the façade. It houses precious pictorial works reproducing for the most part "Mythological scenes and characters" and several "Hunting scenes" which are particularly delightful. The paintings in the *tablinium* (the reception room of the house, normally situated between the atrium and the peristyle) with a mythological subject have been transferred to the Museum in Naples.

This page and opposite above, views of the House of the Classical Hunt, a typical atrium residence which had probably just been rebuilt and decorated at the time of the eruption. On the walls are splendid frescoes of hunting scenes, cherubs, Mercury in profile (below left).

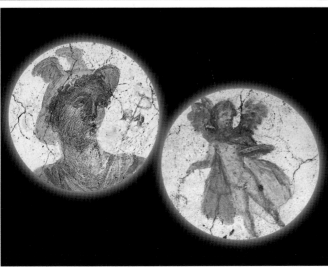

23 THE ORPHEUS CROSSROADS

The main crossroads of Pompeii, the *quadrivi* where four main thoroughfares of the city met at a right-angle, usually had a fountain offering a pleasant little resting place as well as being a vital point for the supply of water. This was the case of the Orpheus Crossroads where Via del Vesuvio, Via di Nola, Via Stabiana and Via della Fortuna all met. The most famous fountain remains however, the one with the cornucopia which gave its name to Via dell'Abbondanza.

24 HOUSE OF ORPHEUS

The great painting on the wall at the end of the peristyle lands its name to the house. This gigantic painting represents Orpheus taming the wild beasts with his lyre.

25 HOUSE OF LUCIUS CAECILIUS JUCUNDUS

Built on the threshold of the 2nd century B.C. in limestone from Sarno and with decorations in tufa stone, in 79 A.D. this residence belonged to a wealthy banker, Lucius Caecilius Jucundus who kept his rather interesting archive here. Some 154 wax tablets have survived with the sums he paid to those for whom he acted as an agent to sell goods (especially slaves) or collect rent. The house also contained two famous relief sculptures (one stolen and the other in storage) showing the damage caused to some public buildings in the city by the earthquake of 62 A.D.

Left, the fountain at the Orpheus Crossroads. Below, Via del Vesuvio, with pedestrian crossings made from blocks of lava as high as the pavements to avoid contact with the waste water where there were no drains. On the right, above, the impluvium in the House of Orpheus and a bust of Lucius Caecilius Jucundus; centre, the wall painting of the mythical singer; below, a relief from his house.

26 TOMB OF CAIUS VESTORIUS PRISCUS

Just outside Porta Vesuvio, a short distance from the walls, there is a group of four tombs, of which the most important is that of the *aedile*, Caius Vestorius Priscus. This walled tomb is painted inside with scenes from the life of the dead man.

27 CASTELLUM AQUAE
(WATER TOWER)

Near Porta Vesuvio the water coming from the acqueduct of Serinus was collected in this reservoir and from here the distribution of water around the city was regulated. Located at the highest point in Pompeii (42 m.) the downward slope was exploited to increase the pressure of the flowing water, which was regulated by a series of sluice gates.

WATER SUPPLY IN THE CITY

The supply of water in the city had always been a most important factor in the busy and prosperous life of Pompeii. The oldest and most generally used method was doubtless the collection of rain water. Every house was equipped with a *compluvium*, an opening in the roof of the atrium, for this purpose as well as drains through which the water flowed into a basin, the *impluvium*, from where it reached an underground cistern which fed the well. The distribution of water underwent a substantial and extraordinary increase with the construction of the Augustan aquaduct: from the springs of the Acquaro river on Mount Serino, water was brought to the *Castellum Aquae* from which three main pipes distributed it to crossroads where water towers were situated, with lead tanks that provided the supply and regulated the pressure. From here the abundant, fresh water reached 40 public fountains, as well as providing spectacular lily ponds and private baths in the houses of the wealthy.

Center, the tomb of Caius Vestorius Priscus and, below, the Castellum Aquae. Above, a fresco that illustrates a table set with a valuable silver service.

Left, views of the House of the Golden Cupids named after the portraits of Cupids in gold, located in one of the cubicula. Beside, the intriguing remains of an obsidian mirror.

Below, frescoes in the House of the Vettii: "The child Hercules killing the serpent" and the frescoes that decorate the "lararium", the domestic temple of the Lares. Below left, one of the statues that decorated the peristyle.

28 HOUSE OF THE GOLDEN CUPIDS

This particularly sumptuous and elegant dwelling belonged to the Poppei family. Its state of preservation - the house has recently been restored - permits full appreciation of the pictorial arrangement as well as of the well-balanced and harmonious architectural layout.

It takes its name from the decoration depicting "Cupids" situated in one of the *cubicula*: the graceful figures are painted on gold leaf. A fairly recurrent feature in this house is the presence of theatrical masks.

The peristyle - perhaps the most beautiful part of the house - is partly raised and almost takes the form of a stage: this reveals a certain tendency by the owner to search for new and effective design which, however, is not lacking in sobriety and elegance. This space was perhaps intended for theatrical representations, as can be deduced from the presence of a flight of steps and three entrances.

Worthy of note is the decoration of several rooms, for the most part belonging to the III style, and having "Mythological episodes and characters" as their subject.

Among the interesting curiosities to be seen here are the temple dedicated to the cult of the Egyptian goddess Isis - very rarely found in Roman society - one dedicated to the cult of the Lares and finally the remains of an obsidian mirror.

29 HOUSE OF THE VETTII

This provides a most precious record of Pompeian painting and is one of the most beautiful and interesting houses in the town. The excellent state of preservation allows us, from a distance of centuries, to appreciate the magnificence attained in the dwellings belonging to the wealthiest class in Pompeii and to observe how the rich local middle-class tended to display their prestige and high standard of living by their extravagant construction of sumptuous buildings, equal, if not superior, in terms of decorative richness, to those of the aristocracy. The house

The salon or triclinium of the House of the Vettii, rich freedmen with cultural interests, is famous for the panels painted in a warm "Pompeian red" and the sophisticated friezes representing a band of merry cupids occupied in games and work. Above are the delightful wine-maker cupids with a row of amphora; below gold-maker cupids are busily fusing and weighing with their scales. Right, below, cupids intently preparing perfumes; above, fresco with a scene of a naval battle, beneath a theatre mask and items used in the cult of Dionysus.

A reconstruction of the verdant peristyle of the House of the Vettii and on the right, one of the elegant courts with an impluvium which face on to it. Above right, more frescoed walls of a room with the scene of Pentheus killed by the Baccantes.

of the Vettii belonged to Aulus Vettius Restitutus and to Aulus Vettius Conviva, and expresses as few others do, the economic position which they had attained at the end of the 1st century A.D. The execution of a large part of the pictorial decoration, a dazzling testimony of painting in the IV style, should in fact be attributed to the period after the earthquake of 62 A.D.

The various rooms and their cycles of paintings merit examination in detail. The dwelling has remained virtually intact, or has been minutely renovated, and this contributes to the unique atmosphere and impression of stepping back into the past.

In the entrance is "Priapus", a very common pornographic figure in Pompeian houses, in that it symbolized fertility, but most importantly served to ward off evil influences from the house. The decoration of the atrium takes "Cupid" and "Psyche" as the subject. There are also two safes here where the owners kept their valuables.

The roof has been completely rebuilt so as to recreate the most accurate picture possible of the time, as well as a highly evocative atmosphere.

The rooms which open off the atrium contain paintings showing mythological scenes, some of which are very interesting in terms of their expressive immediacy.

There is a magnificent peristyle, which skilful renovation has restored to its original form, even as far as the vegetation typically present in these small courts is concerned. It is a rare

complex in terms of charm and the admirable fusion of architectural, sculptural and pictorial, as well as naturalistic, features.

The triclinium is the room which has become justly famous for its paintings.

They almost entirely cover the walls (one part has been lost), are on a red background and the depictions are incorporated into mock panels. The large scenes reproduce mythological characters. "Perseus and Andromeda", "Ariadne and Dionysus", "Daphne and Apollo" and "Neptune and Amymone". Of particular interest is the long frieze which runs round the walls: it contains images in miniature depicting "Cupids intent on various activities", and is of the most refined workmanship. In detail they represent: "Cupids at target practice, Cupids with garlands of flowers, Cupids selling perfumes, Cupids with chariots, goldsmith Cupids, Cupids manufacturing cloth, Cupids celebrating sacred rites, Cupids gathering grapes, Cupids celebrating Bacchus and Cupids selling wine". The large fascia lower down bears depictions of "Psyche" intent on weaving garlands of flowers and "Mythological scenes".

Other rooms show exquisite pictorial decoration, for the most part belonging to the IV style. A room in the east section contains pictures representing "Daedalus and Pasiphae" and "Ixion being tortured", together with large fascias decorated with marine flora and fauna. In another room in the same section there are paintings with mock architecture enclosing depictions of "Hercules killing the serpent", the "Torture of Dirce" and the "Torment of Pentheus".

A novel feature here are the servants' quarters and the kitchen in particular which allow for a reconstruction of domestic life.

oration is very fine and particularly outstanding is that on the walls in the reception area which perhaps provides, one of the most important examples of painting in the II style, characterized by admirably executed mock architecture. In the course of the renovations undergone over the years, the house was equipped with a system of private baths and its own shop for the grinding of grain and for baking bread.

☰ HOUSE OF THE FAUN

The dwelling is of remarkable proportions, harmonious and well-balanced in its design, while its various rooms are elegantly decorated.
It represents the classical type of Roman house. Undoubtedly it belonged to one of the most prominent local figures - the nephew of Silla who dealt with the political organization of the city.
Its original structure dates to the Samnite

☰ HOUSE OF THE LABYRINTH

This house, which takes its name from the subject of the mosaic, "Theseus in the labyrinth", dates back to the Samnite period, as can be inferred from the style and from the Tuscan atrium in particular. Another atrium, the one which opens out after the entrance to no.10, is tetrastyle. The pictorial dec-

Above left, the House of the Labyrinth; below a view of the House of the Faun.

PLAN

1 - Main entrance
2 - Second entrance
3 - Tuscan atrium
4 - Tetrastyle atrium
5 - Tablinium
6 - First peristyle
7 - Exedra
8 - Second peristyle

This page, the main atrium of the magnificent House of the Faun as it is today and how it would have looked at the height of its splendour, before the eruption, in an ideal reconstruction. In the centre of the atrium, in the impluvium, there stood, and still stands today, the famous little bronze figure (now a copy) after which the house is named.

One of the most famous mosaics of all antiquity came from the House of the Faun and is now in the National Archaeological Museum in Naples. The "Battle of Issos" is exceptional in terms of its size (measuring altogether 3.5 m. x 6 m.) - but also in its expressive power: it shows a throng of soldiers, lances and horses captured at the moment when Alexander the Great, by now the victor, is about to inflict the decisive blow on the troops of Darius III, king of Persia, who are already fleeing. This mosaic paved the *tablinium* and in the 19th century it was removed and transferred to the museum collections of the Bourbons. Today, however, it once again embellishes the House of the Faun, as a copy that exactly reproduces the original (consisting of over two million tesserae and one thousand supporting panels) has been placed in the original site. The copy was commissioned by the Archaeological Superintendency of Pompeii and was made by the International Centre for the Study and Teaching of Mosaics in Ravenna.

period, during the 5th century B.C.; its present-day arrangement should be dated to the transformations of the 2nd century B.C.

The Tuscan atrium belongs to the first period and has a stone floor. The second atrium is, on the other hand, of the Hellenistic type and has four Corinthian columns.

Its reputation and name are linked essentially to the little bronze of the "Dancing Faun" found here, a small masterpiece of ancient statuary.

Also quite remarkable, however, is the mosaic now housed in the Archaeological Museum in Naples showing the "Battle of Issos". This mosaic paved the *tablinium*.

Among the rooms particularly worthy of mention are the two peristyles: the first has an Ionic colonnade partly decorated with stuccos and with a magnificent exedra, which is also decorated with mosaics, the subject being "Flora and fauna from the Nile region".

The second, the larger of the two, has a Doric colonnade disposed around the garden.

32 TEMPLE OF FORTUNA AUGUSTA

Built in the 1st century B.C. at the command of the politician Marcus Tullius, the temple is characterized by a pronaos embellished with elegant columns placed above a staircase.
At one time there were several statues in the cella, including one in honour of the Emperor Augustus.

Opposite page: more views of the House of the Faun.
This page: an ideal reconstruction of the Temple of Fortuna Augusta and the remains as they appear today.

33 HOUSE OF BACCHUS

On the Via del Foro, not far from the Temple of Fortuna Augusta and the Forum Baths, is the House of Bacchus, consisting of some quite interesting ruins. Among other artefacts found here is an unusual spatula made of bronze and perforated with holes – a unique example of a tool that was in use some two thousand years ago.

View of the House of Bacchus and, above, the bronze spatula found there.

34 FORUM THERMAL BATHS

These were established in the 1st century B.C. under Sulla and were the only ones still in use after the earthquake of 62 A.D. They consist of two sections, for males and females, both divided into *frigidarium*, *tepidarium* and *calidarium*. The heating and cooling system of the rooms was achieved by running pipes through the cavities in the walls. All the rooms are elegantly decorated. In the male section - this is the better preserved part - the rooms used for changing are still recognizable, as is the *frigidarium* with its circular plan enlivened by large niches (it is embellished with stuccowork and paintings); in the *tepidarium* a magnificent barrel vault worked in plaster and a series of telamons (statues leaning against pillars) interspersed with rectangular niches can be seen; finally, the *calidarium* is barrel-vaulted with an apse at the back. The part of the building which looks out onto the street contains workshops.

Below left, a view of the entrance to the Forum Baths which are reproduced in the plan, below right.
Right, two more views of the interior of the large complex of the Forum Baths with the calidarium above, and the tepidarium below.

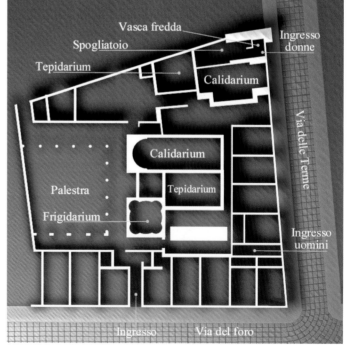

Vasca fredda
Spogliatoio
Tepidarium
Ingresso donne
Calidarium
Calidarium
Via delle Terme
Palestra
Tepidarium
Frigidarium
Ingresso uomini
Ingresso
Via del foro

35 HOUSE
OF THE ANCHOR

This stands at the beginning of Via di Mercurio, after passing under the Arch of Caligula.

The mosaic of an anchor found in the entrance, as can be seen in the picture, gave the name to the house. The anchor symbol was probably linked to the owner's occupation.

36 CAUPONA
IN VIA DI MERCURIO

This is a type of bar-restaurant. The room immediately calls to mind moments of everyday life in ancient Pompeii, thanks above all to the freshness and spontaneity of certain small pictures which are found inside and which, with extreme simplicity, offer a glimpse of the activity involved in this business specifically, and the life of the past in general.

Above, Via di Mercurio showing the perfect paving, and the entrance to the House of the Anchor with the famous mosaic.
Right, the wall frescoes of the hostelry or "Caupona" in Via di Mercurio, seen below.

Furnished with a peristyle which has a pool, elegant porticoes and sophisticated Corinthian capitals, the House of Meleager must have been a luxurious and richly decorated residence as can be seen from the images here.

37 HOUSE OF MELEAGER

This was built in the Samnite epoch, but transformed, especially as far as the decorative part is concerned, in the following era.

Especially lovely is the room used for receptions, characterized by an elegant colonnade with Corinthian capitals.

There is also a delightful peristyle with a colonnade which follows the perimeter of the central pool.

38 HOUSE OF CASTOR AND POLLUX

The dwelling consists of a number of smaller houses, renovated at one time or another and merged into one. Of particular interest is the atrium where a magnificent colonnade with Corinthian columns stands out, as does the pictorial decoration of several rooms, including the series of pictures with mythological scenes depicting "Apollo and Daphne", "Adonis", "Silenus" and "Scylla". The House of Castor and Pollux, or of the Dioscuri, owes its name to the depiction of the "Dioscuri" which decorated

the entrance and which is now housed in the National Museum in Naples, together with other paintings which once embellished the other rooms.

39 HOUSE OF THE CENTAUR

The entry from Via di Mercurio represents the merging of several houses into one.

40 HOUSE OF THE FIGURED CAPITALS

This residence belonged to a noble family. Its construction dates back to the Samnite epoch, as can be appreciated by the sober and severe architectural design.
Of particular interest are the sculptures of the capitals which are now housed in the Pompeii Museum. These depicted "Bacchanalian scenes".
Also worthy of mention is the Lararium and the sundial in the garden.

41 HOUSE OF THE BLACK WALL

An elegant and refined dwelling characterised by a magnificent decoration on a black background - hence its name - with small painted putti representing Cupids. The peristyle is very elegant and distinguished by columns decorated with plaster.

42 THE TOWER OF VIA DI MERCURIO

The walls of Pompeii were punctuated by square towers. The best evidence of this is provided by Tower XI, which rises at the end of Via di Mercurio.
The tower was built by the Samnites, and preceded the siege by Sulla in 89 B.C.

43 HOUSE OF APOLLO

The structure and the materials used bear witness to the fact that this dwelling belongs to the most ancient type and that, at a later stage, it was embellished with decorations in the IV style. The name derives from the depictions of "Apollo and Marsyas" which decorate the walls of a *cubiculum* where mock architecture, reminiscent of the structure of a theatre, can also be found. The mosaics situated outside this room are of considerable interest as are those which once embellished the fountain.

44 HOUSE OF ADONIS

The building takes its name from the marvellous painting entitled "Adonis wounded" which is one of the most beautiful and interesting examples of ancient painting.

From top, the peristyle of the House of Castor and Pollux, the Tower of Via di Mercurio and the House of Apollo.

It occupies one of the garden walls and is incorporated in the midst of paintings with a landscape theme. Other paintings depicting "The Toilet of Hermaphroditus" decorate one of the rooms looking out onto the same garden.

45 HOUSE OF THE SMALL FOUNTAIN AND 46 HOUSE OF THE LARGE FOUNTAIN

The fountains that adorn both these houses are absolute masterpieces of the art of mosaic work.
The one in the House of the Large Fountain consists of a niche which is completely covered with polychrome tesserae. It is embellished with a bronze statue and theatrical masks.
These nymphaea, made of glass paste stones, are rare examples of mosaics other than for floors or pavements.
Of additional interest is the pictorial decoration in the first of the two houses, which contains some delightful small pictures inspired by the landscape.

The characteristic and splendid nymphaeum fountains that decorated the House of the Small Fountain (left, and below left) and the House of the Large Fountain (below). Decorated with mosaics and enhanced with sculptures, they represent some of the most remarkable examples of a decorative element that became popular about the middle of the 1st century A.D.

adjacent to the dwelling leads us to suppose that the owner was involved in commerce. At the entrance is the characteristic "Cave canem" (beware of the dog), one of the best-known images from Pompeii. The depiction of the "tragic poet" was found in the *tablinium* and has given its name to the dwelling and several paintings. The series of paintings in the *triclinium* take as their subject scenes from mythology: Theseus and Ariadne and Venus and cupids. Other paintings with a mythological subject decorate the walls of the *cubicula*. There is a very fine fresco showing the "Sacrifice of Iphigenia" now housed in the Archaeological Museum in Naples. Some experts have identified it as a copy of the work by the famous Greek painter Timante of the 5th century B.C.

47 THE "FULLONICA"

The activity of the fullers was quite widespread in Pompeii. In this fulling mill (*fullonica*) the cloth, linen and sheets were stretched out in the sun between supports designed for the purpose, after having been immersed and washed in the vats under the portico. The bleaching was carried out in specially-made tubs.

48 HOUSE OF THE TRAGIC POET

Its name derives from the mosaic scene depicting a "Master of the theatre". It dates back to the imperial age and is luxurious and refined, especially in terms of the fine decoration of some of the rooms. The architectural design is composite and harmonious: it is of modest but well-balanced proportions. The presence of workshops

Views of the harmonious and aristocratic House of the Tragic Poet; finely decorated and enhanced with elegant architectural features, it is particularly famous for the large mosaic in the entrance with the image of a guard dog, reinforced with the inevitable motto, "Cave canem".

49 HOUSE OF PANSA

A building of vast proportions, to the extent that it alone occupies the whole of insula no. 6. The original structure dates back to the Samnite period. Subsequently the dwelling was divided into a series of small rooms intended to be let, as is evident from an inscription to this effect and by the presence of an independent entrance to each of these small apartments. The conversion of this building is proof of the changing needs of Pompeian society which, in the 1st century A.D., passed from being a primarily agricultural economy - the inhabitants of the houses were land-owners, as is indicated by the presence of the plot of land behind the house - to one based on enterprise and commerce. There is a beautiful Tuscan atrium (part of the original construction) and a peristyle which is laid out around a pool. Behind it open out the rooms set aside for service purposes, including kitchens, latrines and a building for housing vehicles as well as the area intended for use as a vegetable garden.
The original decoration has been completely lost.

50 HOUSE OF SALLUST

An interesting construction of the Samnite epoch, as demonstrated by the Tuscan atrium with its jutting out roof sloping towards the *impluvium* to facilitate the collection of rainwater. The decoration is primarily in the form of plaster work and belongs to the I style.
Some rooms show evidence of renovation and paintings of a period subsequent to the date of construction. One such example was the fresco depicting the myth of Actaeon assailed by dogs which enhanced the garden.

51 HOUSE OF THE SURGEON

This name derives from the series of surgical instruments found here, now housed in the Archaeological Museum in Naples, the nature of which leads us to suppose that a doctor lived here.
The structure corresponds to the oldest type of house in Pompeii, both as regards the architectural design, the distribution of the rooms, and the materials used in its construction (4th-3rd century B.C.). The simple and severe façade is covered with stone slabs.

Above, an ideal reconstruction of the painting of Actaeon assailed by dogs, in the House of Sallust. Right, an external view of the House of the Surgeon.

The surgical instruments of iron and bronze, such as probes, gynaecological clamps, catheters and scalpels found in the House of the Surgeon provide some information about the state of Roman medicine in early Christian times. It was deeply influenced by the expertise of Greek medical practice and used substances obtained from herbs and medicinal plants, though surgeons operated on wounds, broken bones and tumours. Oddly enough, many surgical instruments have been found in several houses in Pompeii.

52 PORTA ERCOLANO

The gate has three arches, two of which were reserved for pedestrians. Its construction dates from the Roman period, but another much simpler gate previously existed on the site. Opening onto the north-west stretch of the city walls, it also provided the most important access to Pompeii. Its other name was Porta Saliensis, in memory of the fact that it was from here that the carts transporting salt used to travel.

53 STREET OF THE TOMBS

Along the Street of the Tombs is a vast cemetery area which is the most impressive and most important of all those which stood on the outskirts of the city. The feature of greatest importance is the presence of a complex of dwellings, villas and workshops which, in terms of number and quality, constitute a veritable town. This feature confirms the enormous expansion which Pompeii underwent at the height of its splendour, to the extent that suburbs, which were well organized from every point of view, sprang up outside the traditional boundary wall. As a consequence, this section of the city can also be said to have played a role of primary importance, both from the socio-historical and urban point of view. The street, apart from villas such as those belonging to Diomedes and to Cicero, and the one known as the Villa of the Mosaic Columns, is also flanked by numerous workshops.

Below, a view of the Street of the Tombs, a typical long street and, on the right, an ideal reconstruction of how it must have appeared before the devastating eruption of 79 A.D.

THE SEPULCHRES

These are of various types and forms: small temples and exedrae, altars or commemorative stones and mausoleums. Funerary objects and decorations of artistic merit have been found in many of these. Among the most interesting and outstanding sepulchres are: the sepulchre of the priestess Mamia, that of the Istacides (characterised by a raised temple on a podium), of Terentius Maior, one named for the "blue vase" (after the magnificent vase found here and now housed in the Museum in Naples) and that of Umbricius Scaurus (it contains admirable images of "gladiator games"). Each sepulchre, whether large or small, bears the name of the deceased or of the family who owned it. Often their business is indicated and the event which made them famous is commemorated.

54 VILLA OF DIOMEDES

This villa is without doubt one of the masterpieces of Pompeian architecture, especially in terms of the unusual design of the building. Indeed, though it maintains certain important features of the Roman-type house, it is laid out with an eye for space and light and above all is arranged over various floors, following the natural inclination of the terrain, resulting in the building being constructed in an airier and more original way. This residence, situated along the Street of the Tombs, is of vast proportions. The principal nucleus has an equally enormous garden, surrounded by a long colonnade which creates a porticoed space and is furnished with a pool.

The rooms lie on one side of the garden itself and are in their turn arranged around a peristyle which communicates directly with the outside. Worthy of particular attention is the large apsed room, characterized by its airiness and the extensive view which it enjoys. There is a beautiful open gallery which also shares views of the gulf, as does the terrace, which at one time lay along the whole length of the colonnade. At the corner of the entrance to the villa are the baths furnished with a small pool. A series of little steps links the staggered floors to one another, creating further interest. One of these staircases leads to the *cryptoporticus*, that is to say the underground rooms of the dwelling.

Eighteen bodies were found in this house, a further reminder of the disaster which struck Pompeii in 79 A.D.

The villa was brought to light in the second half of the 1700s and thought – albeit arbitrarily – to be the house of Arrius Diomedes because it was situated opposite his tomb.

An aerial view showing well the complex structure of the Villa of Diomedes, a huge building enhanced with a vast garden.

Built about the 2nd century B.C. on the slope facing towards the coast, the Villa of Mysteries is similar to the more than one hundred villas that have been discovered in the area around Vesuvius. Generally they were associated with an agricultural use of the land, but also reflect the tendency of wealthier families to build a second home outside the city, often designed using the most fashionable Greek architectural and decorative features.

55 VILLA OF MYSTERIES

This villa stands right on the outskirts of Pompeii, beyond the archaeological area proper.

Grandiose in its proportions and famous for its magnificent fresco cycle, it has, since the discovery of the first rooms, created great excitement among the experts owing not only to its complexity and the particular features of its architectural design, but above all for the precious pictorial cycle and for its interpretation, connected with the religious cults which existed alongside the official religion. The villa was built around the 2nd century B.C., but was renovated and embellished in the imperial age, an epoch in which it assumed the splendid appearance which is still recognisable today, even if somewhat impoverished by the

loss of certain furnishings and many precious ornaments as a consequence of the earthquake of 62 A.D. when it was abandoned by its owner.

The architectural design

The villa has a square plan. To make it conform to the irregular and uneven terrain on the site, unlike the villa of Diomedes which overcame the problem by means of a complex organization of its structure and linking stairways, the Villa of the Mysteries was supported on a base created on a specially made embankment, so that the whole house could lie on a single level, thus facilitating a very regular and well-balanced construction. In addition, a long colonnade and a series of gardens unite the building with its surrounding environment, creating a

truly delightful and harmonious whole. The entrance to the villa is through an exedra, a sort of bright veranda open towards the outside, on either side of which are two *viridaria* (terraces with garden) and two colonnades. The tablinium and the atrium follow: the first contains a splendid pictorial decoration on a black background and delicate miniatures (III style).

The *cubicula*, the rooms next to the atrium, contain magnificent decorations in the II style with daring use of perspective.

On the part at the back an airy peristyle opens up with sixteen Doric columns. Beyond it are the courtyard and service rooms.

The villa is equipped with two ovens and rooms for wine-making. Several rooms are furnished with bathing facilities.

THE PICTORIAL CYCLE: "CYCLE OF THE MYSTERIES"

The first impression gained on entering this room is one of sheer amazement. The walls are covered with an absolute masterpiece of painting: life-size figures tower up in the frescos and the outstanding use of that shade of "red" known as "Pompeian" admirably unifies the various scenes. The long line of depictions unravels freely without any break in continuity. Although at first it might be impossible to grasp the meaning behind the paintings, they still succeed in communicating a sense of something great and mysterious all the same. Although the experts do not all agree on an interpretation of the meaning of the "Cycle of the Mysteries", fundamentally they all recognize it as referring to the initiation rites to the Mysteries of the cult of Dionysus. This cult was forbidden by the Roman government because it was thought

to bring about disorder and was considered to be remote from the state religion, though it was especially deeply-rooted in southern Italy, where it was easier to escape the watchful eye of the Eternal City. The cycle of paintings in the villa must therefore be seen not only as an important record of pictorial art, but also as an exceptional proof of the survival, in the suburbs, of the Dionysiac rites. The scenes shown in this room – adhering to the interpretation which has gained most consensus among the experts who have tackled the problem – probably depict the initiation rites at the marriage of a bride, probably the lady of the house, identified by some as the veiled figure in one of the panels.

Reconstruction of the narrative cycle:

1st scene: the young Dionysus reads the sacred ritual, while a seated woman listens and another, standing, follows the reading:

2nd scene: a young girl bears offerings; a seated woman, helped by two youths, purifies herself;

3rd scene: Silenus plays the lyre, while a woman offers milk to a fawn;

4th scene: a terrified girl takes flight (notice the cloak which billows up owing to the young woman's haste);

5th scene: Silenus offers water to a young Satyr, while another holds up above him a theatrical mask;

6th scene: the wedding ceremony of Dionysus and Ariadne;

7th scene: a woman keeps the symbol of fertility hidden behind a cloth, while a winged figure strikes with a whip a young woman who is leaning on another's lap (flagellation was part of the rite of initiates);

8th scene: the dance of a Bacchante;

9th scene: the future bride prepares for the rite;

10th scene: a seated woman observes the whole scene; this is perhaps the portrait of the lady of the house, she herself an initiate in the Dionysian rite. Regardless of the meaning of the individual episodes, what is most striking is the masterful orchestration of the whole and the narrative capacity of this unknown artist, who, with powerful synthesis and a strong pictorial sense, has succeeded in admirably rendering the mysterious atmosphere which governed the rites of the god. The density of colours and the ceaseless flow of the figures, as well as the balanced formulation of the whole cycle, make this an unforgettable masterpiece.

The rooms in the rest of the villa are decorated with paintings in the II style.

The section which contains the kitchens, baths and storehouses is most interesting, as is the *cryptoporticus* where small and narrow windows create a unique contrast between darkness and light. Many corpses were found in the villa, taken by surprise during the appalling tragedy.

The VIII Regio occupies the south-west of Pompeii and consequently the area of Porta Marina, Porta Stabia and the Holconius crossroads. It includes the area of the Triangular Forum and part of the buildings situated in the stretch of Via dell'Abbondanza between the Holconius crossroads and the Civic Forum. This is the ancient heart of Pompeii, massed around the area of the original triangular-shaped Forum, the nucleus of the social, political and economic life of the town before it became one of the most important and rich commercial centres in the region.
Characteristic of this area is the irregular nature of the terrain which influenced the layout of the streets and structure of the houses. Indeed the whole of the VIII Regio stands on steeply sloping ground, on the extreme edge of the lava terracing on which the city was founded. The streets are not in an orthogonal grid typical of Roman town planning and the houses, in order to adapt to the natural difference in level, often have two storeys, their design enlivened by open galleries and stairways.

56 PORTA DI STABIA

Its name derives from the fact that it connected Pompeii with Stabiae. Set into the ancient and mighty walls and providing an opening in the southern stretch, it is perhaps the oldest gate in the city. The deep imprints left on the paving of the street which passes through it bear witness to the heavy traffic with which it had to contend. On its far side is the beginning of the Street of the Tombs.

57 TRIANGULAR FORUM

The name derives from the area's triangular shape. The outer edge reaches as far as the confines of the lava terracing and consequently looks out over the plain below. As mentioned above, the Triangular Forum represents the original social and political centre of Pompeii, and as a result can be said to belong to the Samnite epoch. The entrance is made up of *propylaea* characterised by a fine colonnade in the Ionic style; a fountain stands alongside. The inside of the square is bordered by another colonnade in Doric style - there are an astonishing 95 columns - while one side has a panoramic view towards the sea. In all likelihood the colonnade was originally used for gymnastic activities. In the centre of the area stands the Doric Temple, and consequently the sacred area which extends around the temple itself, with three altars in tufa stone from the pre-Roman age and a sacred well. The pedestal standing in front of the entrance bore a statue of M. Claudius Marcellus, nephew of the Emperor Augustus.

Above left, the entrance to the Triangular Forum and, left, an ideal reconstruction showing the Doric-style colonnade and the large Doric Temple. Above, a view of the Triangular Forum.

GENERAL LOCATION PLAN

1 - Large Theatre
2 - Odeon (Small Theatre)
3 - *Quadriporticus*
4 - Doric Temple
5 - Triangular Forum
6 - Samnite Palestra
7 - Temple of Isis
8 - Temple of Jupiter Meilichios

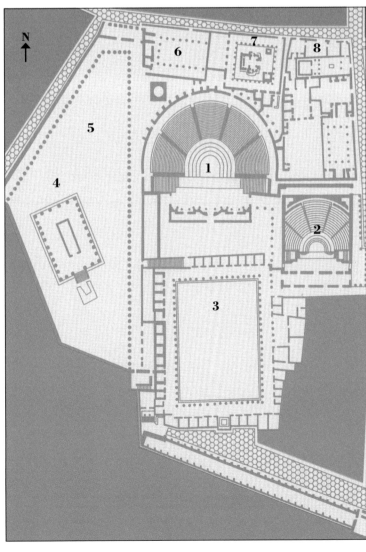

58 DORIC TEMPLE

This is among the oldest in the city and probably dates back to the 6th century B.C.: it was dedicated to the cult of Hercules who, tradition has it, was the founder of the city. Subsequently the goddess Minerva was worshipped there too.
The pedestal and the staircase which gave access to it are all that remain of the building.
Only fragments such as column drums and parts of capitals belonging to the renovation work which the temples underwent now remain.

59 SAMNITE GYMNASIUM

Constructed in the Samnite epoch this was the centre for the gymnastic activities of the Pompeian nobility until the much larger gymnasium situated on the outskirts of the city near the Amphitheatre was created. It has a rectangular plan flanked on three sides by a colonnade and is surrounded by high walls. Its proportions were reduced at the time of the construction of the Temple of Isis. The architectural layout is extremely plain. It was here that the beautiful statue of the "Doryphorus" (lance bearer) was found; it is now housed in the National Archaeological Museum and represents one of the masterpieces of ancient art. It is a copy of the more famous statue by the Greek sculptor Polycleitus.

60 TEMPLE OF JUPITER MEILICHIOS

This rather small building became the principal seat of the cult of Jupiter and the Capitoline triad Jupiter-Juno-Minerva, when the larger temple of Jupiter on the Forum square was destroyed in the earthquake of 62 A.D. Fragments of the statue of the lord of Olympus were found among these very ruins. It is adorned with a large tuffaceous altar.

Views of the remains of the once magnificent Doric Temple, with the stairway that has remained almost completely intact.

61 TEMPLE OF ISIS

This is a real jewel of Greek architecture and one of the best preserved buildings in Pompeii. An inscription informs us that the temple was restored in order to remedy the damage suffered as a consequence of the earthquake of 62 A.D.: this has certainly contributed to its present state of preservation, as can also be said for the beautiful pictorial decoration which has now been removed and is housed in the Archaeological Museum in Naples.

The building consists of a large rectangular space surrounded by walls, within which is the cella of the god raised up on a pedestal and standing in a splendid niche. Of great elegance and interest is the small temple - with its plaster decorations - situated in the peristyle and used for the preservation of the Nile water considered to be holy by members of the cult of the Egyptian goddess Isis. Adjacent to the temple there is also a space to accommodate the priests' houses and for the faithful to meet.

62 SMALL THEATRE OR ODEON

Established in the 1st century B.C., it represents one of the most harmonious and well-balanced examples of architecture of this type. It could hold up to 1,000 spectators and could be covered permanently. It is well preserved and shows the typical design of the Greek theatre with its structure deeply embanked in the natural slope of the terrain.
It was used to host plays and musical events as well as for the performance of mimes.

63 LARGE THEATRE

This is a magnificent building constructed in the 2nd century B.C., with the stage area subsequently undergoing conversion. As a type it conforms to the Greek theatres in that the architectural structure adapts to the natural inclination of the terrain. During performances it could be covered, but it was not equipped with a permanent canopy, a privilege enjoyed by the Small Theatre. It had a remarkable capacity, being able to hold up to 5,000 spectators. Comedies and tragedies were performed here. A special feature of this theatre was the natural background which could be used as scenery: there is in fact a panoramic view across to the splendid circle of mountains which stand behind Pompeii. In the southern area of the Theatre there was a colonnade intended to accommodate the spectators during the intervals or at the end of the performance.

Views of the rather well-preserved, elegant Small Theatre.
Pages 84-85, the magnificent and spectacular Large Theatre.

Mime was a special theatrical performance of a comical or even bawdy nature, inspired by aspects and incidents of everyday life.

Usually it only lasted for a short time.

The actors used masks as a rule and women were also admitted to the performance, which was not otherwise the case.

Mime originated as farce in Sicily and was later developed in the Roman age.

Reconstruction of the Large Theatre

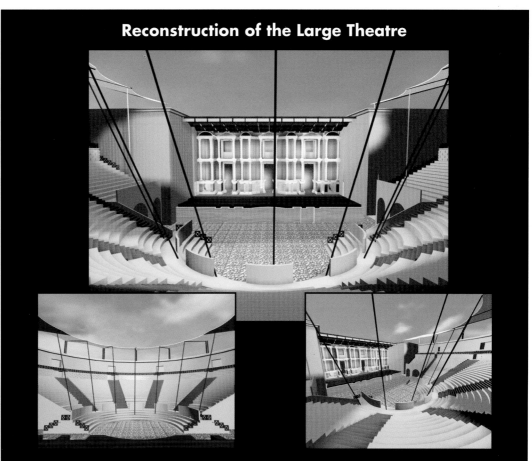

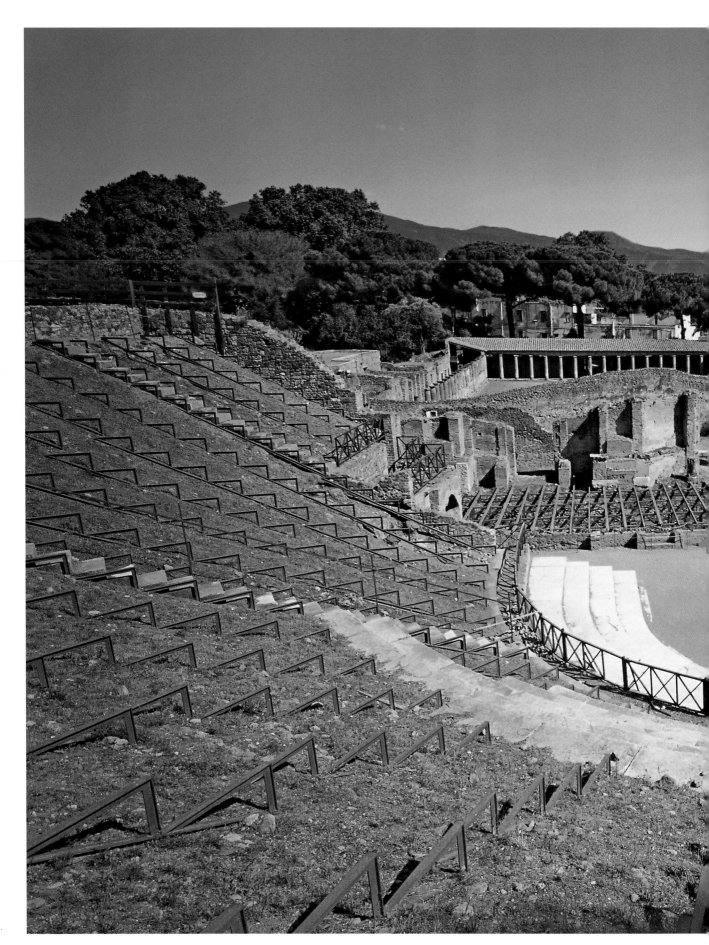

64 GLADIATOR'S BARRACKS

This very ancient building was closely connected with the Theatre, since originally it provided a meeting place for the audience during intervals in the performances.

Under Emperor Nero it was used as the gladiator's barracks, a suitable place for providing accommodation and a practice area for those men who were employed to fight. It has a square plan preceded by an entrance and columns. Around the perimeter runs a colonnade of 74 columns. It consists of two floors and includes in addition, storehouses, dining rooms and sleeping quarters. The numerous weapons found during the excavation work are housed in the Archaeological Museum in Naples and provide extensive documentation of great interest.

65 HOUSE OF CORNELIUS RUFUS

This stands opposite the Baths; it must have belonged to the Gens (family) of the Corneli. Quite impressive are the peristyle and its fountain, the large marble *impluvium* and most especially, the lovely and sombre portrait of the owner of this elegant residence.

66 HOUSE OF HOLCONIUS RUFUS

It belonged to one of Augustus' tribunes, a prestigious personage of the age.
The house is spacious and elegant.
The remains allow us to guess at the architectural structure, which must have been particularly beautiful in the area of the *tablinium* and the peristyle, characterized by an airy open gallery. Refined pictorial decoration covered a large part of the walls of the house.
Adorned with fountains and a cycle of paintings, the summer *triclinium* would have been particularly delightful.
The frescos, which must once have been splendid, are now only partly visible as a result of deterioration: they depict "Mythological scenes and characters".

67 STABIAN THERMAL BATHS

These occupy a vast area between the lane of Brothels, the Holconius crossroads and the Via Stabiana. They represent the oldest thermal complex in the city. They were, in fact, built at the time of Pompeii's subjugation to Rome and were subsequently extended and decorated on more than one occasion to more adequately fulfill the needs of the growing population.
The original construction, situated in the northern part of the building beyond the colonnades, is of the Samnite period. The more recent part - dating to renovation during the Roman age - overlooks the western side: it is organized according to more modern and functional criteria.
The thermal complex consists of a well-constructed system of baths distributed around a central area used as a gymnasium and characterized by a colonnade ranged around three sides of the building.
The Stabian Baths are composed of three parts: the rooms in the north section, the oldest as mentioned above, contain a series of latrines.
The second section consists of a group of private baths situated behind the northern colonnade. The third section is located on the eastern side: it consists of changing rooms, a vestibule - with magnificent plaster decoration - rooms for the cold bath (*frigidarium*), for the tepid bath (*tepidarium*) and for the hot bath (*calidarium*).

The Thermal Baths are rigidly divided between the area set aside for men and the area for women. Both are organized in the same way, but the female section is simpler and has fewer decorations.

A pool occupies the western side of the Baths.

The rooms are frequently adorned with stuccowork of fine craftsmanship and certainly among the most beautiful in Pompeian art.

It is also possible to identify the system used to heat and cool the various rooms, which was achieved by pipes carrying air and water of varying temperature through the cavities in the walls.

In the third section the public baths are equipped with a pool and rooms used for practising gymnastic activities.

Pages 88-90 and 91 above: views and, on the left, an ideal reconstruction of the large porticoed central court of the Stabian Baths, splendidly decorated just before the eruption of 79 A.D.
It was used as an open-air gymnasium where combat exercises often took place.

68 HOLCONIUS CROSSROADS

This represents the junction of the major Pompeian thoroughfares: the Via dell'Abbondanza and the Via Stabiana. The name derives from the statue of Holconius Rufus, an illustrious personage of the town, which at one time was placed at the base of the arch that stood here. On one of the corners is a fountain bearing the symbol of the Concordia Augusta.

At the Holconius Crossroads (below) the remains of a pillar with a hoist to distribute water throughout the area can still be seen, as well as the four pillars that supported the four-vaulted arch.

69 HOUSE OF CASCA LONGUS

The group of workshops which occupies part of insula no.6 belonged to a single owner, a certain Casca Longus who had his house built in close communication with the shop. On the walls of the atrium a delightful decoration showing scenes related to the theatre can be seen, and in one of the rooms is another painting of floral motifs. The house owes its name to the inscription borne by the *trapezophori*, (the statues which support the table), and probably belonged to the Casca Longus who was one of the protagonists in the conspiracy which led to the assassination of Caesar.

70 HOUSE AND WORKSHOP OF VERECUNDUS

This is an extremely interesting complex in that it provides an example of a typical workshop belonging to the sellers and dyers of cloth, an activity which in Pompeii was particularly well developed and so important that a building in the Forum square was dedicated to them - the Eumachia Building. Precious paintings embellish the workshop and depict both the protector gods and the activity carried out there.
Of particular interest are: "Mercury with a moneybag", "Venus on a carriage", "The cloth sellers" and "The weaving of cloth", all of which are depicted with great immediacy.

71 HOUSE OF THE CITHARIST

This is one of the largest houses in Pompeii and is made up several houses merged into one.

The name derives from the statue depicting "Apollo Citharist" found here and housed in the Archaeological Museum in Naples, as is one of the beautiful animal sculptures in bronze that functioned as water spouts on the peristyle fountain.

The house has recently been restored and now we can still imagine the magnificence of the internal architecture of the house and the richness of the decorations which once made it splendid.

Of great spectacular effect are the three overlapping peristyles.

Here, and on the following pages: the House of the Citharist is renowned for the splendid decorations in the peristyles and the statues that embellished them, including one of Apollo Citharist and the famous figure of the boar being savaged by dogs.

of special clays, then trampled
again and immersed once
more in basins of water
to remove any impurities it
may have accumulated.
The cloth was finally carded,
shaven, dyed and stretched
in special presses.

72 FULLONICA STEPHANI

This is one of the best preserved work-shops in Pompeii.
The *fullonicae* were the laundries. Observation of the interior of the workshop allows us to reconstruct all the stages of the treatment of cloth, from washing, to pressing, to drying and dying.
The Fullonica Stephani (Stephanus was the owner's name) also contained a spacious room to accommodate customers.

The Fullonica Stephani, a workshop where cloth was treated.

THE TREATMENT OF CLOTH

The cloth was first immersed in large vats where it remained to soak for some time, together with substances which helped to remove the grease (urine and soda). Next, it was put into other vats where it was rubbed and trampled underfoot.
In the following stage the cloth was softened by the use

The imposing Doric columns surrounding the impluvium of the atrium in the House of the Diadumeni, also known as the House of Marcus Epidius Rufus.

73 HOUSE OF THE LARARIUM

A room near the *tablinium* and commonly known as the Lararium shows refined decoration with depictions of "Scenes from the Iliad". The blue colouring of the background is interesting and creates an intensely atmospheric effect. There is a large painting in the so-called Hall of the Elephants. From an examination of the plastered walls and the material found in the rooms, we can deduce that, at the moment of the catastrophic tragedy, the house was in the process of being decorated.

74 HOUSE OF THE CRYPTOPORTICUS

It takes its name from the *cryptoporticus* - a room of startling effect thanks to apertures which allow shafts of light to filter in - which was the underground cellar of the house, used for storing wine. It contains an exhibition of plaster casts of people who died during the eruption of Vesuvius. The house also contains pictorial decoration related to the II style. It consists of "Episodes from the Iliad" incorporated into a frieze (in the colonnade). In addition there are some admirable caryatids painted in red, and still lifes.

75 HOUSE OF THE DIADUMENI OR OF MARCUS EPIDIUS RUFUS

This large house was built in the Samnite period about the second half of the 2nd century B.C. and must have belonged to Marcus Epidius Rufus or to Marcus Epidius Sabinus as can be deduced from the frequent appearance of these two names in electoral propaganda found posted on the façade and on the walls of the nearby buildings. Externally a two-step podium, a rather unusual architectural element, runs along the façade. Beyond the entrance hall lies a large Corinthian-style atrium where sixteen columns with Doric capitals surround the central pool of the *impluvium*. Of all the various Corinthian atriums known in Pompeii (those with a series of columns around the sides of the *impluvium*), this is the most important. Various rooms are arranged around this, but in a departure from the classical layout, the wings are at the centre of the side walls instead of at the back. They are preceded by a pair of Ionic columns and the corner pilasters have capitals decorated with the heads of maenads and divinities.

In the wing on the north-western side is an apse which, as an inscription with a dedication on the podium indicates, was built by two freedmen called Diadumeni (giving this name to the house) in honour of the Lares and Geni of their master, Marcus, clearly one of the two public figures mentioned above.

76 HOUSE OF MENANDER

This is one of the largest and most elegant houses in Pompeii, very rich in its decoration and highly complex in the division of the rooms. The house has recently been restored. Its name derives from the portrait of Menander, but is it also known as the "house of the silverware" because of the copious collection of pieces found in a chest in the cellars of the house: a total of 118 pieces of silver, as well as numerous others made of gold, and coins. The house belonged to the Poppei family and underwent various phases of building. Begun in the 3rd century B.C., it was later extended and embellished; at the moment of the eruption of Vesuvius the building works were still underway. From the entrance - distinguished by two pillars with Corinthian capitals - access could be gained to the atrium (of Tuscan type), which is fairly well preserved and quite atmospheric thanks to the decoration in the IV style, the charming little temple placed in one corner and above all because it preserves intact its jutting out wooden roof open at the centre to allow light to pass through and facilitate the collection of water. The rooms to the left of the entrance contain paintings showing scenes representing "Episodes of the Iliad". Beyond the *tablinium* is the peristyle, an elegant and refined room with its beautiful painted colonnade. A series of rooms leads off from here: on the right is the kitchen and bathroom area; on the left is the *triclinium* flanked by two rooms with frescoed walls. The exedrae situated

Below, the House of Menander: the bathroom with a mosaic floor and the fresco with a portrait of the poet. Right, the House of the Ceii: frescoes with hunting scenes.

beyond the rooms set aside for servant accommodation contain refined paintings of a mythological and theatrical nature (masks) and the portrait of the poet Menander mentioned above. The western area of the house is occupied by the quarters set aside for use as bathrooms: there is a fine *calidarium* whose mosaic and pictorial decoration is virtually intact. One section of the house was reserved for the curator of the property, a freedman called Eros (we know his name from the seal found on his body), who safeguarded the goods in the house and bore the title of procurator.

77 HOUSE OF LUCIUS CEIUS II OR HOUSE OF THE CEII

The house stands along the lane which leads to the right from Via dell'Abbondanza. Its name is taken from the electoral inscriptions found on the front of the house. This dwelling is distinguished by the panelled decoration on the façade. It has a precious tetrastyle atrium. Inside are several ornaments and some furniture - particularly noteworthy is the cast made of the wardrobe - as well as the staircase which joined the ground floor to the upper storey. In the garden a delightful picture depicting animals and plants can be admired.

78 HOUSE OF THE LOVERS

This house, albeit of modest proportions, is an architectural jewel. The decoration of the walls shows great refinement and the peristyle surrounded by a double open gallery is truly delightful. The ceilings and floors of several of the rooms are intact. In the atrium is a collection of friezes, panels and painted medallions.

A painting of Paquius Proculus with his wife, housed in the Archaeological Museum of Naples.

The name of the house derives from an inscription which refers to the sweetness of love and states that "lovers, like bees, wish life to be as sweet as honey".

79 HOUSE OF PAQUIUS PROCULUS

Paquius Proculus was a very influential political figure in Pompeii. The building shows evidence that it was extended at different times. The decoration in the atrium of geometric squares with figures of animals is highly sophisticated. The *tablinium* has a fine alabaster floor. The pictorial decoration has also partially survived, with remains of still lifes, and the dog on the chain placed to guard the house. The cryptogram which has been found bearing the Pater Noster Cross must be a Christian sign of recognition. In the age of Nero (when the Christians were persecuted for their religious beliefs), a skilled dramatist succeeded in arranging the 25 letters of the Pater Noster Cross and the

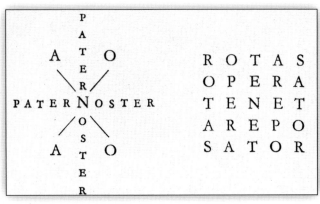

```
        P
        A      O
    A   T
      \ E /
P A T E R N O S T E R
      / O \
    A   T      O
        E
        R
```

```
R O T A S
O P E R A
T E N E T
A R E P O
S A T O R
```

symbol A.N.Ω. into a remarkable rebus which rapidly spread
throughout the Christian world.
The symbol means Our Lord is
the Alpha and the Omega of all
things. The single middle N is
common to the two symbols.

Above, the Pater Noster cryptogram found on a fragment of plaster in the house of Paquius Proculus and one of the mythological scenes frescoed in the House of the Priest Amandus. Left, statue of the Ephebe found in the house named after it and now housed in the Archaeological Museum of Naples.

80 HOUSE OF THE PRIEST AMANDUS

In the fine *triclinium* is an admirable series of paintings with mythological subjects: "Hercules", "Polyphemus", "Perseus" and "Daedalus and Icarus". A painting of the pre-Roman period can also be found near the entrance. There is a noteworthy plaster cast of a tree in the garden of the peristyle.

81 HOUSE OF THE EPHEBE

The house takes its name from the statue of the Ephebe, a bronze copy of a similar Greek work dated 5th century B.C., found here and transported to the Museum in Naples. It is a very large house and sumptuous both in terms of its architectural design (it consists of three houses merged into one), and the decoration which characterises it. This confirms that it belonged to a family of the rich middle-class who were keen on an ostentatious display of their high standard of living. Of the paintings preserved here, that of "Venus and Mars" is most noteworthy. The marble covering of the floors is quite remarkable - the one in the *triclinium* is particularly precious in that it was executed with rather rare coloured marble - as is that of several walls. Among the objects found here are four statuettes - the *placentarii* - which were used as sauce boats and which are characterized by their provocative nature (Museum in Naples). Worthy of attention is the adjoining small house where some outstanding paintings embellish the *tablinium*, having as their subject "The marriage of Venus and Mars".

The thermopolia were where drinks were sold. The one named after Asellina - one of the names written on the plaster on the walls - is perhaps the best preserved in Pompeii: apart from the stone counters with holes in to hold the amphora for pouring drinks, it preserves ornaments, containers for hot drinks and a good many bronze vases.

The names of the women written on the walls of the workshop and the presence, on the upper floor, of numerous small rooms, has led to the assumption that the owner of the *thermopolium* ran another business as well, perhaps not just a mere sideline, which consisted of managing a house of pleasure.

WORKSHOPS AND BUSINESSES

Pompeii provides ample documentation on the type of workshops which existed in ancient times and consequently on the various activities carried out in the town. There are the *fullonicae*, which are the workshops of the textile workers (see Fullonica Stephani and the series of rooms in insula 6, nos. 6-12, whose interiors contain all the working tools and the tanks used for dying and manufacturing cloth); the *thermopolia*, in other words, the equivalent of modern-day bars with counters for serving drinks. There are a good many *tabernae* which correspond to the inns of today. Bakeries are widely represented, equipped with mills for grinding grain, as are breadmakers' (*pistrinum*) warehouses for storage and counters for the sale of bread. There are also plenty of shops selling fruit and vegetables and garum, the latter being one of the favourite sauces of ancient times, as well as workshops belonging to the cloth, wood and iron craftsmen. In general, all the shops bear insignia on the façade, showing the symbol of the owner's category or trade; inscriptions and graffiti are frequently found, which not only indicate the name of the workshop, but also provide a list of materials and notes on the merchandise.

The bars and taverns of ancient Pompeii can be identified from their unusual furnishings, such as the typical counters with a place for the amphora used for pouring out the drinks.

83 HOUSE OF TREBIUS VALENS

The name of the owner is present in an inscription in the bedroom. Its façade was once covered by inscriptions which almost certainly served as public announcements.

Inside is an admirable peristyle with an unusual pictorial decoration of geometric motifs and a *triclinium* furnished with fountains and a pergola.

One bedroom contained a collection of small bottles for ointments and jewels, which leads to the supposition that the room belonged to the owner's wife.

84 HOUSE OF THE ORCHARD

It owes its name to the pictorial decoration showing "Trees and fruit" which adorns some of the rooms, one of which has a blue background and one black. They are paintings of extreme freshness and refined elegance.

Several types of trees (fig, plum, cherry, arbutus and lemon) are faithfully reproduced; in the fascia below, a delightful garden is depicted. Some experts have connected these paintings with the Dionysian cult; others, more simply, have imagined that the owner was a fruit-grower.

Above, the House of the Orchard: a detail of the elaborate painted decorations with a theme of scenes from nature.
Left, and on the opposite page, views of the House of Loreius Tiburtinus, with a large garden and the nymphaeum flanked by frescoes of mythological scenes (opposite, below right, Pyramus and Thisbe and below left, Narcissus at the fountain).

85 HOUSE OF LOREIUS TIBURTINUS

The house of the magistrate and priest of Isis, M. Loreius Tiburtinus; on the feast days of the cult of Isis, the waters of the fountain imitated the flooding of the Nile.

The house underwent two phases of construction: the first relates to the area within the Tuscan atrium (Samnite epoch); the second, centred around the peristyle area, may be attributed to the imperial age.

The house is distinguished by its magnificent garden consisting of an open gallery and a pergola embellished by water channels, fountains and a temple as well as by pictorial decorations and sculptures.

More views of the House of Loreius Tiburtinus where the splendid verdant garden was enhanced with loggias and pergolas, as well as a little temple, situated above channels that brought water to feed the numerous fountains.

The mythological depictions bear the signature of their author, a certain Lucius. Precious paintings adorn the *triclinium* ("Episodes from the Iliad").

Other paintings, for the most part belonging to the IV style, decorate one of the small rooms next to the large hall.

An interesting feature is provided by the cast made of the great entrance portal to the house. The combination of the decoration and the architectural layout of this house bear witness to the prestige and affluence of the family who lived there.

86 HOUSE OF THE VENUS MARINA

This was the residence of a wealthy family, as can be deduced from the richness of the materials used and from the decorations. Apart from the fresco depiction of "doves, fountains and flowers", there is a remarkable large fresco of "Venus in a sea-shell" on the garden wall. The scene is delightful in appearance: the goddess is riding through the waves in a shell escorted by Cupids. The fresco is peopled with birds and flowers. On one side is a depiction of the god "Mars in armour". Other rooms contain paintings including the particularly fine ones on a black ground. The house has recently been restored.

The impluvium of the atrium and the peristyle of the House of the Venus Marina showing the elegant grooved columns.
Following pages, the spectacular frescoes, the loveliest of which is the portrait of Venus that has given the house its name, and the reproduction of a statue of Mars in armour that stands in front of a fantastic garden filled with birds.

Gardens, orchards and vegetables

Apart from the petrified image of a dead city, recent interesting initiatives in Pompeii have helped to bring back to life a living and vital element that arises, however, from the past. The gardens and orchards of the ancient city have been revived with their original layout by the Archaeological Superintendancy. As a result of careful studies, the plants that embellished the gardens of ancient Pompeii flourish once more, alongside those introduced during the excavations of the mid-18th century to enhance the archaeological area. Thus, since 1999, in the area around Via dell'Abbondanza, two authentic nurseries have been created occupying two gardens that in ancient times adjoined the House of Pansa and a house in the Regio VIII. The choice of plants grown depends on two basic concepts: firstly, the most common essences found in ancient Pompeii have been collected following identification through study of the plants seen in the frescoes, as well as pollens, seeds and woods found in the surrounding

area. The second element is provided instead by "modern" plants, usually used to enhance the boundary of the archaeological area. Among these are aromatic plants (laurel, myrtle, rosemary, lavender, sage, thyme, etc.), fruits (arbutus, pomegranate and quince), and ornamental plants (roses, oleanders, ivy, asparagus, box, and St Peter's palms).

Moreover, in the area around the amphitheatre where in ancient times vines grew, vegetables and fruit trees flourish once more. And naturally the vines have been replanted too, scientifically tracing the modern descendants of old local varieties such as the *Vitis oleogina* and the *Colombina purpurea*. In autumn 2001, after three years of experimentation and vinification trials, the first important harvest of some 20 quintals of grapes took place. The wine produced was aged in oak casks and was bottled about 18 months after harvesting. Thus history has presented us with an excellent wine named the "Villa of Mysteries".

87 VILLA OF JULIA FELIX

This is a magnificent construction occupying the whole of insula no.4: it consists of a villa, a thermal complex given over to public use and a collection of workshops merged into one. The house proper, furnished with two entrances, is spacious and luxurious. At one time it was adorned with paintings, though these have now been removed and are housed in the Louvre Museum.

The garden, enlivened by fountains, bridges and columns is highly atmospheric. In the *triclinium* the beds are made of marble and the bath complex is furnished with every comfort - *frigidarium*, *tepidarium*, *calidarium* and also a sauna facility. It is laid out according to the traditional design of public baths and also includes an outdoor pool.

Initially it belonged strictly to the villa, but was later given over to public use upon payment of a fee, as demonstrated by an inscription to this effect found here. The complex of workshops and rooms situated along the lane to the west was also created by the proprietress with the intention of leasing them out.

At the back of the villa lies a vast area, set aside for the cultivation of fruit and vegetables.

88 PORTA DI SARNO

This gate was constructed in the Samnite epoch and is now in a somewhat deteriorated condition. On the right lies the vast area on which the Large Gymnasium and the Amphitheatre stand.

Villa of Julia Felix: the area of the garden with the portico of grooved pilasters.

SUMMER FESTIVAL IN THE ORCHARD OF JULIA FELIX

Thanks to the strong committment of the Archaeological Superintendency of Pompeii and to a series of specially organised events, it has been possible for this buried city to once again savour the many flavours and aromas once familiar to it, particularly during the summer months. Thus, in addition to meetings and tastings to discover the foods and delights of ancient times, the gardens, orchards and vegetable plots have been recreated, especially the orchard of the House of Julia Felix where the native Vesuvian apricots, much appreciated and justifiably quite famous even some 2000 years ago, abound once more. In fact, the cultivation of apricots and peaches was brought to the slopes of Vesuvius from the east in the first century A.D. and today is still flourishing, even inside the archaeological area.

The orchard of the House of Julia Felix, one of the largest agricultural properties of the urban area, began to surface from its past in 1936 and has gradually been recreated as close as possible to the original, through a scientific study of the position of the roots of trees that have come to light. These roots must, in fact, have belonged to fruit trees but it is possible that vegetables were also cultivated in this orchard.

SOUTHERN ENTRANCE
TO POMPEII - AMPHITHEATRE AND SURROUNDING AREA

89 LARGE GYMNASIUM

This was established in the 1st century A.D. when, owing to the sharp population increase and the great urban development which overtook Pompeii, the Samnite Gymnasium situated in the Forum proved insufficient. It consists of a majestic colonnade, quadrangular in shape, including a large space intended for the practice of professional gymnastics. It also contained a pool. The structure has recently been restored.

90 AMPHITHEATRE

This is an impressive and grandiose construction, capable of holding up to 12,000 spectators (though some have calculated up to 20,000). It hosted all the circus shows and gladiatorial games so dear to the Pompeians, who devoted most of their leisure time to these performances.
The period of its construction dates back to 80 B.C. (it was commissioned by the magistrates Quintus Valgus and Marcus Porcius) and is therefore one of the oldest buildings of this kind in existence, suggesting that it might have represented a model for all those that were subsequently built in Rome.

A view of the external profile of the Amphitheatre, behind which rises the bell tower of the Sanctuary of Pompeii.

It was constructed part-
ly by making use of an
embankment, partly by
digging down into the
earth for several metres.
The access steps are out-
side the building. The
doors on the western side
lead into the arena.
Unlike the other Roman
amphitheatres, the one in
Pompeii does not have
an underground section.
It was equipped with a
velarium, that is a cover
which was stretched over
the complex in case of
rain: the rings to which
the canopy was fixed can
still be seen.

*Views of the portico
of the Gymnasium that
looks towards the Large
Amphitheatre (above).
Right, a reconstruction of the
brawl between supporters
of Nocera and Pompeii,
described by Tacitus, which
caused them to be banned
from the games for ten
years.*

THE GAMES

Various games or *ludi* took place in the amphitheatres. The most common were the *venationes* or hunts: these were fights between gladiators and ferocious beasts. Among the most famous spectacles were the battles between the gladiators themselves. Various schools were set up for the training of these men, who, each time they competed, would stake their own prestige and ability. The gladiators were for the most part slaves and prisoners of war who were seeking to win their freedom by taking part in these combats. The infamous and tragic slaughter of the Christians was perpetrated in none other than this arena.

The performances put on in the amphitheatre sometimes included naval battles and other such competitions. All in all it provided the chief source of entertainment for the society of that time. As a ploy to win the favour of the people and for their own electoral propaganda, the Roman magistrates themselves used to finance the games.

91 GARDEN OF THE FUGITIVES

The name is derived from the garden in which many corpses of Pompeians were found, overtaken by death as they were about to flee from the city. Their "impressions" have been left in situ where they were found. The corpses of the thirteen victims thus provide one of the most vivid and terrible reminders of the disaster.
The land was attached to a type of farmhouse.

92 THERMOPOLIUM OF THE PHOENIX

Unlike the other *thermopolia* in Pompeii, this one has extremely modest features and consists essentially of a place of refreshment situated in the shade of a simple pergola. The location takes its name from the depiction of the phoenix depicted on the shop sign.
Alongside it two peacocks are also painted.

93 GARUM WORKSHOP

This is none other than a sauce factory where the *garum*, which was much used and appreciated in ancient times, was produced. The containers for its preservation can still be seen.

GARUM

This was a sauce made by steeping the intestines of fish such as tuna, mackerel and moray eels. These were chopped, salted and allowed to ferment in open-work baskets, so that the liquid could filter through. It was one of the favourite foods of the Romans and was used as a basic condiment for a number of dishes (see page 33).

THE IMPRESSIONS

These provide dramatic evidence of the city's last living moments. They take the form of casts of people, animals, objects, furniture and even plants, obtained by pouring liquid plaster into the space left in the ground by the disintegration of the solid matter. Their conception was inspired by Giuseppe Fiorelli, one of the originators of the excavation of Pompeii. He realized that as the corpses and objects had decomposed, they had left a vacuum in the ground. This vacuum was carefully cleaned of any residual matter and filled with plaster, which, once set, perfectly assumed the shape of whatever had lain beneath the ashes. After the procedure was finished, the "impressions" were brought to light. The result was a collection of realistic and dreadful images captured in the moment of their demise: the terror-stricken expressions on the faces of the people are haunting, as are the suffocated cries on their mouths. Several of the corpses were caught in the act of embracing one another, almost as if to stave off the calamity; some were caught as they were trying to flee; others were surprised in the act of rescuing valuable objects and money from the cataclysm.

Above, a view of the House of the Ship Europa. Right, a glimpse of the garden of the Perfumer's House.

94 HOUSE OF THE SHIP EUROPA

The house derives its name from the graffito image on the north wall of the peristyle, portraying a merchant ship with the name "Europa" (a clear reference to the mythical heroine abducted by Jupiter in the form of a bull). Access to this large garden was, and still is, from the peristyle where once flourishing vegetables, vines, lemons and fruit trees grew. It is not surprising then that some 28 terracotta pots were found around the boundary walls, containing seeds and shoots. Lastly, at the end of the garden was a stall where the animals of this small farm belonging to the owner of the house were raised.

95 HOUSE
OF THE GARDEN OF HERCULES
(OR OF THE PERFUMER)

The structure of this house is an unusual example of the normal layout of residences in this area of the city: an entrance with bedrooms on either side, which led to a courtyard that is similar to a real atrium. From the courtyard a corridor, with various rooms on either side, lead into the garden. And it was indeed the garden that became the most important element in these dwellings, both in size and magnificence. In the case of this house, the vast garden at the back was organised in the middle of the 1st century B.C. in the place of five pre-existing residences. As a result of

some recent, thorough studies it has been possible to ascertain that in ancient times the plant species cultivated here were normally used to produce perfumes, thus suggesting that the owner may have been a perfumer. The reference to Hercules is based on the marble statue of the god found here together with a tabernacle, also dedicated to the cult of Hercules, and located in the garden. Other features found in the garden are an altar and a stone-built *triclinium* for meals outside.

Further views of the extensive garden of the Perfumer's House showing some interesting and complex architectural features, but also the renewed and lush vegetation.

96 PORTA NOCERA AND THE TOWN WALLS

This was constructed in the pre-Roman age and then rebuilt at later dates. It is located in the southern stretch of the walls of Pompeii, along the uneven lava spur which makes access particularly awkward.

97 NECROPOLIS

The vast area occupied by the cemetery was partly brought to light only a short time ago. The tombs are numerous and of various types: worthy of particular mention are the sepulchre of Eumachia, that of the Gens Tillia and that of Serapius, a Pompeian banker.
In addition, the tomb of the *duovir* Cellius and a truly monumental one belonging to Agrestinus Equitius can be identified, commissioned for the latter by his consort Veia Barchilla.

Views of Porta Nocera (which, due to the later sinking of the road level, appears to be rather high), of the limestone and tufa walls that flank it, of Via Nocera and the tombs of the nearby necropolis.

THE CULT OF THE DEAD

In Roman cities the presence of large, monumental necropoli mainly arises from the great importance that was attached to the cult of the dead at the time. By law, burials had to take place outside the city walls and consequently were concentrated along the main roads leading out from the city gates. The ritual of cremation was in use for a long time and ashes were collected in special urns which were then placed inside the tombs. In addition to the funeral itself, a series of purification and expiation rites took place, marking the days of mourning (usually nine) and also including funeral banquets. There was also a specific period of the year when public and private ceremonies and commemorations dedicated to the cult of the dead took place. This was known

as the *Parentalia* and corresponded to the dates between 13 and 21 February of the contemporary calendar. As for the tombs, as time passed these became increasingly monumental, though this was not only intended to emphasise the immense affection and complete devotion represented by such celebration of the dead.

In fact, they eventually became a reflection of the social position of the deceased and his family and consequently of the rank and role which they enjoyed in society. Thus the necropoli of the 1st century A.D., including therefore this one at Porta Nocera in Pompeii, had become genuine monumental complexes.

98 CENTRAL THERMAL BATHS

This magnificent complex was constructed immediately after the earthquake of 62 A.D. (in fact many of the materials used were plundered from nearby buildings) and was interrupted as a result of the eruption in 79 A.D. It was built on more modern and functional lines than the Stabian Baths, and had to answer, given the dramatic population increase, to the growing needs of the citizens. They are in fact bigger than all the other baths, occupying the area of an entire insula, and are equipped with a large gymnasium, numerous baths and a room intended exclusively as a *sudatorium*. The decoration is the richest and most magnificent in style.

The principal feature of these baths is the way in which their architectural design differs from others: they were in fact designed to be more spacious compared to previous ones and, thanks to the large windows which open out (*calidarium*), are much lighter. In addition, the divi-

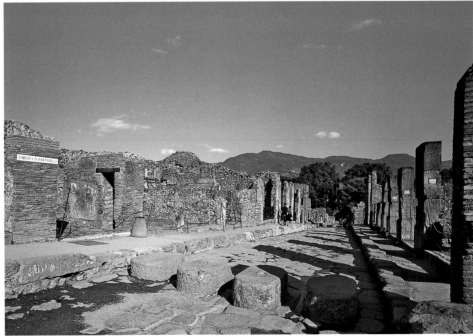

sion between the female and male sections was done away with.

99 HOUSE OF MARCUS LUCRETIUS

This belonged to a Pompeian nobleman who held, among other responsibilities, the office of priest of Mars.

It is an elegant construction whose rooms were finely decorated with pictures now housed in the Museum in Naples. Those remaining show decorations with imaginary architectural buildings, as well as mythological scenes, depictions of "Cupids" and a large painting representing "Bacchus". There is a charming garden area, raised compared with the rest of the house, and embellished with statues, niches and fountains.

Above, an external view of the Central Baths and right, a view of the populous area where they stood.

This page, views of the House of the Silver Wedding, a splendid example of a gentleman's residence in the imperial period, sombre and classic but splendidly decorated. Right, the House of the Centenary: medallion painted with a frescoed landscape.

100 HOUSE OF THE SILVER WEDDING

The house takes its name from the fact that the remains were brought to light on the occasion of the silver wedding of Umberto and Margherita of Savoy (1893).
It is one of the finest examples of a gentleman's residence: the architectural design is extremely sombre and classic, the decoration magnificent.
Executed in the Samnite epoch, it was renovated in the early 1st century A.D. Worthy of particular attention is the atrium consisting of a colonnade of the Corinthian order, grandiose in proportions and soaring dynamically upwards. The rooms